CW00375999

Valley Boy goes West

MEMOIRS OF A PARISH PRIEST

Alan Meats

**Grosvenor House
Publishing Limited**

All rights reserved
Copyright © Alan Meats, 2014

The right of Alan Meats to be identified as the author of this
work has been asserted by her in accordance with Section 78
of the Copyright, Designs and Patents Act 1988

The book cover picture is copyright to Moori

This book is published by
Grosvenor House Publishing Ltd
28-30 High Street, Guildford, Surrey, GU1 3EL.
www.grosvenorhousepublishing.co.uk

This book is sold subject to the conditions that it shall not, by way of
trade or otherwise, be lent, resold, hired out or otherwise circulated
without the author's or publisher's prior consent in any form of binding or
cover other than that in which it is published and
without a similar condition including this condition being imposed
on the subsequent purchaser.

A CIP record for this book
is available from the British Library

ISBN 978-1-78148-730-3

Alan Meats is a native of Pontypridd in South Wales, a town often called "The gateway to the valleys." He began his working career as a teacher but after 7 years in the profession decided to train for the priesthood of the Church in Wales. All his ministry has been spent in various parts of South Wales, the past 25 years in the Llanelli area. In 1994 he was appointed a residential canon of St. Davids Cathedral. His first publication was an adaptation of the memoirs of a Victorian parson entitled, "Llanwynno – A treasury of memories", which describes the life and times of his home area in the middle of the nineteenth century. He and his wife, Gwendoline, now live in retirement at Burry Port, Carmarthenshire.

Lorraine

Every blessing,

Alan J. Meats

October 2014

Dedication

I dedicate this book in commemoration of Corporal Francis John Meats and Sergeant Richard George Prothero, my two grandfathers, who died while serving their country in World War1.

"Grant them, O Lord, eternal rest, and let light perpetual shine upon them."

CHAPTER 1

TOFFEE DABS AND DOUGHBOYS

They say that you are essentially what you are brought up to be. It would appear that there are many notable exceptions to this statement. One only needs to think of the aristocratic Lord Stansgate, Anthony Wedgwood-Benn, who relinquished his peerage to become Tony Benn M.P. and a tireless campaigner for the working classes of this country. It is the word, "essentially" that gives the game away. By this word we mean "that which makes you tick", the ideals to which you steadfastly cling, the personal dreams that you always hoped would be fulfilled. I believe that these things are very much coloured by the way in which you have been nurtured. Furthermore to dismiss as of little consequence the causes and effects of one's formative years would be to ignore a basic and lasting ingredient in one's character. In my case, there is something about the ambience and culture of the South Wales valleys of the 1940's and 50's in which I grew up that undeniably leaves its mark on those who have been cradled in its embrace. That culture even had a language all its own. *"I saw her now just down by the Post Office."* *"What she needs is to move herself, she's so "dedoreth" about the house!"* (*"dedoreth"*, for the uninitiated, means "lazy") A family are about to have a meal round the kitchen table, so the dog is told to go and "cwtch" in the corner, out of harm's way. These and many more such odd turns of phrase were part and parcel of the "Wenglish" that crowded in on my ears as a child.

I am a true Taffy and proud of it! At the same time I am not so proud of the image of the Taffy served up by the familiar nursery rhyme dating from the middle of the eighteenth century intended by some English gentleman to stir up anti-Welsh feeling at the time:

Taffy was a Welshman, Taffy was a thief,
Taffy came to my house and stole a piece of beef;
I went to Taffy's house, Taffy wasn't in;
I jumped upon his Sunday hat and poked it with a pin."

The rhyme goes on to describe Taffy as a sham and a cheat! With my hand on my heart I must confess that the composer of this rhyme lost the plot with regard to describing the "Taffy" population of my acquaintance as a child.

My birthplace was in fact the village of Rhydyfelin, about two miles south of Pontypridd and ten miles north of Cardiff, where the River Taff reaches the sea. Pontypridd is often referred to in the tourist trade as "The gateway to the valleys". It is in fact the confluence of the Rhondda and the Taff, with the Cynon joining forces with the Taff a few miles further north towards Merthyr Tydfil. At Trefforest, on the other side of the Taff from Rhydyfelin, lies the sprawling campus of the University of Glamorgan. When I was a youngster the original building was called the Glamorgan School of Mines, promoted in the 1960's to the Glamorgan Polytechnic, before receiving its present full university status. I was born in my grandmother's house (my paternal grandmother) because during the war years my parents, who had married at the beginning of the war, had not had the opportunity to set up home following my father's being called up for military service! – which was a common enough situation then.

What is your very first memory, I wonder? Mine was the sight of the hitherto undreamed of prize of a Red Label Bournville bar of chocolate that my father brought me when he came home from leave during, I think, 1944. No! This was not the start of the slippery slope of a chocoholic! Personally I can take or leave this item of confectionery as the mood dictates. However that one chocolate bar, so unexpected, acted like a ray of sunshine through the dark clouds of World War 2. Yes, I was a war baby! I once recall mentioning during a Remembrance Sunday service that certain vague memories of the War come back of me as a child, prompting a very audible whisper from the lips of a junior chorister, *"He's talking about the Boer War!"* There was a fierce exchange of words in the vestry after the service between vicar and chorister, I can tell you! After the war I have clear memories of using the gas masks, kept for sentimental reasons in the sideboard, as playthings with my brother, Wayne. We really played the part of being under threat of the enemy! Such is the stuff young boys are made of! One notable domestic scene which sticks in the mind is of my mother (whose reputation for reprimanding us when needed far exceeded my father's) giving Wayne a thorough "dressing down" for tearing a ten shilling note into pieces which he assumed was another piece of brown paper left in the drawer. In 1946 this was an amount not to be discarded so wantonly. But then my brother was only three and already a good rummager! For my part,

I was always in my mother's "bad books" for being "too lazy to catch a cold". If she were in a better mood, she might modify her comments by telling me to "get some more elbow grease" The first time this was said I obediently and misguidedly made my way to the local hardware shop to ask the owner, a bewildered Mr Thomas, *"Please can I have some elbow grease; I am not sure if it is sold in a tin or a bottle!"*

Naturally, like most children, we had our treats each week. The Saturday morning trip to the cinema - mostly to see a Western featuring the exploits of Tom Mix, Tex Ritter et.al. When we came home, it was usually to sample Mrs Hale's toffee apples. Our name for them was "toffee dabs". They came in two guises - the light brown colour or the dark brown. Both varieties were devoured with relish. Being partial to treating all delights equally, I opted to eat each type alternate weeks. At two pence each, who was going to turn his back on a bargain? Besides which, it was my money to spend as I liked - money gained in this way. Every Tuesday I had to run an errand for my Gran which involved taking fresh fish to her friend, Mrs Bramley from Barnsley (the only person whom I knew who spoke with a true Yorkshire brogue). The prize for carrying out this task was two pennies placed decorously in my hand. So my toffee dabs were truly earned!

Mentioning food reminds me of the wholesome quality of our daily diet in those days. My mother was a good cook. Later she was to take on a part-time job as a chef in the local Miners' Hostel, set up to accommodate refugees from Eastern European countries during and after the War. The market in Pontypridd was a popular shopping venue for miles around for its wide range of dairy products, sea food and delicatessen of all kinds. My father had a "penchant" for delicacies that were commonplace then but which would turn many people's stomachs today – pigs' trotters, chitterlings and tripe and onions, for instance. Twice a week, in winter especially, we had either traditional Welsh lamb "cawl" or thick pea soup made with lentils, containing shin beef, or perhaps ox-tail, straight from the butcher's slab. Lovely stuff! These soups were made even more nourishing by the inclusion of what we used to call "doughboys", which are properly called suet dumplings. I do not think I had ever come across the word "dumpling" until I came to read the novels of Charles Dickens. If my brother and I had been especially helpful at home we were allowed two doughboys in the soup. If my mother had forgotten to buy suet to make them you could cut the atmosphere with a knife, such was our dismay that the soup did not contain its crowning glory!

After my father was "demobbed" we set up home about a mile from Gran's but we spent most weekends with her. The old Glamorgan canal from Cardiff to Merthyr (by then largely filled in) ran behind where she lived and, beyond it, an area of common land which was known locally as the "Monkey's Tump", because of its undulating levels of ground. This is where we played "hide and seek" or, more adventurously, we would slide down the slopes on a sledge (a wide wooden plank supported by four home-made wheels) which we called a "bogey". Unlike the "bedroom-oriented play station children" of today, we thrived on the open air. One of my favourite pastimes was playing marbles. I kept my collection of "alleys" of varying colours and sizes and the heavier "bompers" for years afterwards. Had they not disappeared in the throes of moving house some years later, perhaps I would still have them on display today as an heirloom, as I tend to be a hoarder. Pastimes such as "Kick the tin", "Hop-scotch" and skipping with a rope (which boys and girls equally enjoyed) were also popular street games.

While I thoroughly enjoyed playing "touch rugby" and "kick around football" with friends, the game I really enjoyed most was cricket. Unfortunately, whereas you can manage to play several team games on uneven, sloping grounds, you have to have a fairly flat and even pitch on which to play cricket. Good cricket pitches were therefore not easy to find in the valleys! I believe that because cricket is a sport whose intricacies have to be understood in order to appreciate the game, it was the very precise, technical details that somehow attracted me. I am sure that odd phrases such as "silly mid-on", "in the slips", "googlies", not to mention "bowling a maiden over" are enough to make all but the converted switch off! Later in life, due entirely to neglect of the game on my part when school studies took my attention, I relegated my activities to scoring for Wayne's Works team with a very occasional "call-up" to play if a member of the team failed to turn up. My brother was a committed team member for years afterwards and a very competent opening bat, with a distinct preference for the "back foot" (another cricket term!), while I was inclined to be a "front foot" batsman.

We boys kept in good health throughout our childhood, helped by doses of traditional remedies like "milk of magnesia", camphorated oil, and "syrup of figs", as required, and even the dreaded "goose grease" for chesty colds. Inoculations against diphtheria and "small pox" were a regular pattern of life, of course. There had been an isolation hospital for small pox sufferers on the mountain side at Eglwysilan. As a child my mother had been a patient there. As a sign of how times have changed in the field of medicine, one day I heard the sudden rattle of the door knocker. Opening it, my mother greeted Dr Gwyn (we always called the doctor by his Christian name), our family doctor. He had been to prescribe medicine for an elderly neighbour and, as he was so near, had called to see whether "the mumps had cleared from the boys." He then proceeded to accept a cup of tea and engage in a friendly fireside chat. Is this perhaps why today we no longer refer to the doctor as "the family doctor" but as the General Practitioner? Not that today's medics are not just as competent of course, but how greatly has the situation in which they now operate altered.

Tough though the post-war years were with the austere years of rationing, we had our days out from time to time as a family. The most convenient day's "chilling out" was to walk, armed with our picnic, up the side of Eglwysilan Mountain on the east side of the valley. At its top stood the sixteenth century church of Saint Ilan, commanding superb views north towards the southern limit of the Brecon Beacons and south over the Bristol Channel to Somerset and North Devon, apart from the view towards Swansea and the Gower in the west. Even at a young age these mountain walks taught me to appreciate the beauty all around our home and to set it in the context of other areas close by – the whole panorama enabled you to appreciate everything in its perspective of nearby hills and distant sea. Opposite the church was the "Rose and Crown" pub which supplied us with tea and lemonade to wash down the food we had brought, the pick of which were Gran's home - made pasties! My father of course drank something a little stronger. The field behind the "Rose and Crown" was ideal for our ball games. About two hundred yards up the road, down a rough surfaced lane stood the rectory. When I first remember the spot, the Rector, the Revd. Washington-Jones, was still residing there, whether in post or whether allowed to reside there in retirement, I am not sure. He had the care of a parish that included the community of Abertridwr, about a mile away to the east. Like many another feature of church life today, the present incumbent has now taken on the hitherto adjacent parish of Senghenydd – the scene of the horrendous mining disaster of 1913, when so many lives were lost.

For seaside days out it was usually Barry Island by train from Trefforest or the longer journey to Porthcawl, changing at Pyle for the little branch line to the seaside resort.

In springtime we went several times on the little train that went through Saint Fagan's as far as Creigiau to spend a few hours picking primroses and bluebells – made much more desirable as we travelled there by steam train. Once we went by train to Bristol Zoo via the old Caerffili - Newport railway line, which we caught at Rhydyfelin Halt.

Train spotting is a favourite hobby for many boys, and I was no exception. I was favoured in this pastime by the fact that for many years Pontypridd boasted the longest station platform not only in Wales but in the U.K. I spent hours logging the details of each train as it arrived from Cardiff, Newport, Barry, Treherbert, Maerdy, Aberdare or Merthyr. There was scarcely ten minutes to wait before the next train was due. My love of steam trains continues to this day. That all-pervading smell of steam and the homely whistle as she sets off still sends shivers of excitement down the spine – a fond memory now, except for the odd occasion when the "King George V" vintage steam train deigns to rush through Burry Port station on its twice a year trip through South Wales.

When I was about ten years old, the family began the venture of a week's holiday in a caravan at Trecco Bay, near Porthcawl. We thought that the sand dunes were there on purpose to enable us to think that we were trudging through the Sahara Desert or perhaps climbing to the top of Everest! For me, sadly, although today's Trecco Bay has modern amenities we never would have dreamed of as a place to enjoy as children, it takes a back seat to the glorious days of the sand dunes by the sea which so fired our imagination.

In 1950 my maternal grandparents gave me my first taste of the far-off great city of London, We stayed at my uncle's home in Watford and I set myself the task of remembering all the stations from Stanmore into Euston on the Bakerloo line by heart. I can't repeat that feat now! The great attraction for us as visitors to London that year was the Festival of Britain. My first introduction to the Underground system of travel was so striking that I delayed boarding the train, so much was there to take in, that when I tried to enter the train, the doors jammed on me and I thought my end had come! After this ordeal I remember sitting down next to my "Nan" (as opposed to my Gran) and bursting out in a loud, unabashed voice that only impulsive youngsters use shouted, *"Oh, look, Nan, that lady's wearing a much longer dress than Mam's!"*

My amazement at seeing unfamiliar sights often caught me unawares. My first visit to Cardiff saw me introduced to the awesome spectacle of a tram in motion. I was so enthralled at the sound as well as the sight of this strange vehicle with the overhead electric cable that, in following its movement with my gaze, I collided with a lamppost and spent the rest of the day at Roath Park nursing a bloody nose!

Much sentimentality has been engendered through the years about the close-knit lives of the coal mining communities since people sometimes wear rose-tinted spectacles, helped along by the novels of Richard Llewellyn and Alexander Cordell. Yet, above and beyond these outbursts of "hiraeth" (melancholy) for what has been, I can truthfully state that I, for one, was nurtured in an atmosphere noted for its distinctive neighbourliness – in which the phrase "we are all in it together" was a reality not a convenient, political slogan. One local character was typical of this interplay of relationships. She was called "bopa" in the "valleys" community. She was not a relative but a family friend, usually living close by (but not necessarily), who was always on hand to help out in a family crisis. She was always referred to by her surname. Thus "Bopa" Thomas in Number 6 Dyffryn Road would make us children a hot meal if Mam was laid up with the flu. She was a kind of "auntie" who was not an "aunt", but just as helpful. This word seems to be quite unfamiliar to other parts of South Wales.

I grew up in the years when the once thriving coal industry of the valleys was clearly in decline.

The century of belching smoke and scarred hilltops was coming to an end, but not quite finished with. My Gran kept a lodger for some years who was a miner, so the tin bath, hung up ready for use in the scullery, was as familiar an item in the home as carbolic soap. But the days of the sound of the hob-nailed boots clattering down the pavement after completing their subterranean shift were numbered. The first colliery in the area to close was the Albion in Cilfynydd (home village of operatic singers, Sir Geraint Evans and Stuart Burrows) which closed in 1966 and is now the site of the Pontypridd High School. Two collieries were then shut down in the aftermath of the devastating Miners' Strike and subsequent decimation of the coal mining industry in 1984 – namely Nantgarw in 1986 and then the Lady Windsor, Ynysybwl closed in 1988. My uncle was employed in the lamp room of the Tymawr Colliery, Trehafod, now the site of the prestigious Rhondda Heritage Centre, which today is resplendent with en-suite hotel accommodation and restaurant. The "tough as teak" colliers of old would surely shake their heads in disbelief to see their old work-place thus transformed for the pleasure-seeking tourists.

All is change, yet much that still is has in a sense not changed. The society which nurtured me may have given up the ghost of its slag heaps but there is still evidence of a mind-set that steadfastly clings to the old lifestyle which was once familiar. The river Taff, the coal dust acting as a dark shroud, as I watched it flowing down towards Cardiff while waiting for my school bus to arrive, has now been the haunt of anglers for some years as they pursue the salmon that had long abandoned its depths to the sombre blackness.

However, despite the changes to the eye of the modern resident or visitor, there is something changeless about the vivid memories of a childhood in which my Gran would not contemplate locking her door at night, however stormy the weather outside, a childhood in which we knew and spoke to everyone in the street, in which warm relationships were a natural extension of family ties and in which every day when I came back from school I could open the back door and say, "Mam, I'm home!" and receive a welcoming answer.

CHAPTER 2

INFLUENCES AT WORK

Since Gran's house was my birthplace, she was perhaps destined to play a large part in my formative years. Not only was her home my introduction to this world but during childhood my brother and I (he was two years my junior) spent almost every weekend there. This meant that we had more friends who lived in her part of the village than nearer our home, since Saturdays offered the

Glantaff Infants school, Rhydyfelin -
"Where my education began"

best "quality time" to foster friendships for us as children. Widowed since World War One (both my grandfathers lost their lives in that conflict), Gran never re-married, bringing up her two sons, my uncle Selwyn was her elder son and my father, Ted, her younger, during the tough years that followed the Great War and into the General Strike of 1926 with its soup kitchens and the years of the Great Depression that followed. She took in washing and ironing to make ends meet. I remember her telling me how her housework in those days involved ironing and starching the kind of white "overalls" that extended down to the ankles worn by shop assistants employed by the retail stores in Pontypridd. When they were hung up in the front room to air, they presented a ghoulish scene to any visitor. My uncle suffered from emphysema and was forced to give up work in the Tymawr Colliery, Trehafod, at the age of 49. He had worked in the lamp room there. Soon afterwards he started up a business of his own. My father was an apprenticed painter, decorator and sign writer, starting work at ten shillings a week. I was fascinated seeing him graining doors by hand and his training as a sign writer encouraged him to produce elegant handwriting, recalling the monastic script of bygone times. Later in life my parents pooled resources rather cleverly to create cakes of quality to celebrate birthdays, anniversaries and weddings for close friends. My mother, Edith, came into her own with her baking skills and my father excelled with his "professional touch" in decorating. My uncle had one daughter, Frances, who was five years older than me. Because she too spent a lot of time with her Gran, especially after leaving school, we boys looked on her as an older sister. This close relationship was even more natural since my mother was the only child, leaving us with no other first cousins. Frances was born in Trefforest, just a few doors from the home of Tom Woodward, who was later to find fame as the pop singer, Tom Jones. In fact Tom and she were pals in school and, whenever, later in life, he was due to give a concert in South Wales, he would always send Frances a complimentary ticket as a reminder of school days. He never forgot his roots, in fairness, - which cannot be said for all celebrities.

To recall early memories one naturally turns to early schooldays. My formal education began in Glantaff Infants' School. Miss Cuff was our head teacher but the first teacher to make her mark on me was Miss John of Lock Terrace, complete with freckled, genial face and ginger hair. It is strange how special occasions from those far-off days remain with you. The picture I have is of each child in turn seated on Miss John's knee (not permissible today) while a "junior xylophone" was placed in front of us. The challenge was to play the notes that were compatible with some familiar nursery rhyme. This and other "brushes" with the world of music as the years unfolded instilled in me a lively appreciation of music which has always been with me. For instance, I am one of those who can usually pitch a note fairly accurately and know therefore if I or those around me are "off key". In fact my parents were both fond of music; Mam played the harmonium in church and Dad played the ukulele (a kind of guitar) for his own amusement. Both enjoyed singing together the songs of the Music Hall days. Songs from the popular musicals of the 1940's and 50's were among their favourites. Indeed Sunday evening at home after church often took the form of an informal "Karaoke" with my brother and I attempting to join in with the words we knew, which weren't many! Encouraged by my mother, I took up the piano at the age of about eight. Sadly, as soon as homework at the grammar school intervened, the piano took a back seat and the instrument was eventually sold. Mind you, it did not help that my piano teacher lived next door and was able to nag me if she did not hear me practising enough. However the lasting legacy to this introduction to the piano was my ability to read music (Old Notation please! Not Tonic sol-fa!) and the ability to harmonise along with the melody. My junior days were spent at Parc Lewis School in Trefforest. Mr Grey was the head teacher, complete with slick hair-style and a strict but kindly manner. Another member of staff was Mr Tysul Jones, a tall man with dark, curly hair who spoke Welsh. He took us for Games. One item on a school report that comes to mind is the comment, *"This boy shows zeal in this subject"*. I had to ask my mother what the word *"zeal"* meant! She wasn't sure but she said that it sounded complementary! My step-grandfather finally came to the rescue by saying that it meant that I showed enthusiasm for the subject! This brought a smile of satisfaction to my face. I am afraid I cannot recall what subject I was supposed to have shown zeal in! It certainly could not have been Mathematics!

The dreaded Eleven Plus came my way in 1952 - the examination that purported to separate the "sheep" from the "goats". When you consider the matter, it was nonsensical to think that one's whole educational path, possibly the entire direction of one's life, could possibly hinge on success or failure on that one day's performance. My brother refused to try the examination, claiming that *"one egghead in the family is enough!"* (said in a jocular manner not a mocking one). About three months before I was due to sit the examination my step-grandfather, John Howell, died. He was the only grandfather I knew and, even though our acquaintance was short-lived, it was cherished.

He was of farming stock and a native of Narberth in Pembrokeshire Like many another native of West Wales, he came to the valleys of South Wales to secure a job in the tin-plate works which were then in their heyday. My Nan was among the female workforce there for many years. Her insistence on getting up at 5.30 a.m. each morning all her life thereafter was a "throw back" to those years of work routine. My grandfather was elected a local councillor and took a particular interest in educational matters in the community. I remember being taken round the polling booths to sample the atmosphere, not knowing the difference between one rosette and the other, naturally. One thing about him that I heard from many a source was – he never made any glib promises to help those he represented just to make himself popular. It was always, "I shall do my very best, but, if I fail, you will know, and know why." He was a "John Blunt" in manner but he was respected for his honesty enough to get elected each time.

There was a transparent integrity about his character that was obvious to those who had any dealings with him. It seems to me that the political scene today would be much healthier if principle took precedence over courting public image. John Howell was also a deacon at Bethlehem, the local Baptist chapel. He spoke Welsh – the only member of my family able to speak the language. He it was who introduced me to the cultural institution of the National Eisteddfod in 1949 at nearby Caerffili, in the splendid grounds of the Norman castle. The whole dazzling experience was an "eye-opener" for me – the pageantry of the "Chairing of the bard", complete with sword unsheathed over the head of the winning poet, and the amazing spectacle of those druids dressed in long, flowing robes, gave me much to reflect on.

John Howell had an allotment as well as a substantial garden. I enjoyed helping to pick the soft fruit in season, to recognise the blight that harmed them, observe the vegetables as they grew and join him in cursing the menace of the weeds. One memorable hot summer's day we returned home dying to slate our thirst. While I made short work of a large glass of lemonade, I heard loud shouts from the pantry. My grandpa had taken a grateful draught from the bottle on the shelf marked "dandelion and burdock". Unfortunately, my Nan had used the same bottle, when empty, for vinegar, forgetting to remove the label! The atmosphere between husband and wife was not too *"cordial"* for a long while afterwards!

I learned much from my time in the allotment with Grandpa – namely, in addition to the Bible as God's Word for our spiritual edification, the Almighty had given us the glory of his creation for our use, but we must learn that patience was essential to see the fruits of our labours fulfilled.

I shall never forget his last words to me when he knew that his time on earth was short. Ironically, these words coincided with the week during which solemn music was being played on the radio to mark the death of King George the Sixth. I was at Grandpa's bedside.

His breathing was extremely laboured as he caught my hand and whispered, *"Alan, 'machgen i ("my boy"), look after your Nan for me when I'm gone, will you?"* *"Yes, grandpa, I will"*, I replied obediently, baffled by this seemingly unachievable task given me at the age of ten.

Within a week I was crying my eyes out at his funeral which was the first time I had resorted to weeping openly in my life, as we struggled to sing the hymn,

"In heavenly love abiding, no change my heart shall fear" to the tune "Penlan" of course.

My Nan's role was to involve me in duties around the house "to earn my keep", such as feeding the chickens in the back garden and collecting the eggs, which I quite enjoyed. Unfortunately, these duties also included cleaning out the chicken coop when needed, which did not thrill me as much! But then, is not life a question of taking the "rough" with the "smooth?" I recall being seated next to my Nan in chapel and her passing me some Communion wine as a "reward" for sitting quietly during the service (not a very sound theological reason for taking Communion, I believe!)

It was my mother's parents' involvement in the chapel that explained my feeling obliged to attend their place of worship every other Sunday, despite attending my Gran's church Sunday school which appealed more to me, I had to admit. I learned quite young in life to value the priority to be accorded to people you love and respect over personal likes and dislikes. When John Howell died the influence of the chapel in my formative years virtually came to an end, apart from the Anniversary occasions and Singing Festivals. However the insights that I received from being engaged with

another Christian denomination did much to enrich my
ministry later in life, even though I could have sworn
that the hands of the clock above the pulpit turned
much more slowly than those of the clock in our living
room! Perhaps they would have turned more speedily
had the clock in chapel been facing the pulpit instead of
facing the congregation?

Gran was a member of the parish of St. Catherine,
Pontypridd and, although she moved out of town
to Rhydyfelin, she remained faithful to the parish of
the town ever since coming to Pontypridd from
her native Yorkshire. This meant that we boys were
brought up in the mission church attached to the
parish of St. Catherine in which she was heavily
involved as Sunday School Superintendent and General
"Dogsbody". Gran was the sort of person whom
everyone naturally called "Gran", whatever their age
or relationship with her. She was "Gran" to neighbours
as much as to friends. She was baptised Eleanora,
but among the close family she was always called Nell.
She was by nature affable, even-tempered, someone
always thinking the best of others, knowing nothing
about "airs and graces" but remaining "gracious" in
everything. She had known much sadness in her life but
bore no grudges as a result. Nothing seemed to daunt
her spirit of serenity. Having been left a young widow in
the Great War she not only brought up her own two
sons but fostered two orphans for several years in the
1920's. She had suffered quite a chequered childhood
herself, she and her three brothers having lost their
mother when Gran was eleven. This was when she went
to live with an aunt in Newport, Gwent. She was made
of stern stuff yet retained a heart of gold. Even when she

lost her eldest son (my uncle) when she was in her late 70's she did not allow her undoubted grief to overwhelm her to the point of despair.

At a very early age I was introduced by my mother (who played the harmonium) and Gran to Mill Field mission, which was then located near the Humphreys Garage off Mill Street, quite near to the present Mill Field school. An unprepossessing building of zinc, its original purpose was to serve the large numbers of caravan dwellers that lived in the immediate area, who plied their wares in Pontypridd market in the years between the two World Wars. Gradually these residents drifted away to live in houses around the vicinity but many continued to attend Mill Field from habit.

The Mission Church was not solemnised for Holy Communion or weddings and so it was usually the parish church at 8 a.m. for Gran and me after I was confirmed. At Mill Field we had a flourishing Sunday school in the afternoon throughout my boyhood days. The evening service at 6 p.m. was usually taken in the early days by Tom Yeoman, the Parish Reader. He and his wife, Mary, a former Church Army Sister, were my godparents. After Tom died, the evening service was overseen largely by a lay worker called Ron Coley. Ron and Gwyneth Coley and I became great friends and later in life I was privileged to be godfather to their children Adrian and Alyson. Despite the lack of formal training, Ron was a very gifted preacher and an informed Bible student. In retrospect, I learned a lot from his homilies which were full of "substance" and spoken with great conviction. It was through Ron and Gwyneth's influence that I was invited to accompany them to London's Harringay Arena to hear Dr Billy

Graham, the American evangelist, in 1955. A year later I was confirmed by the then Archbishop of Wales, John Morgan. At least at the age of fifteen plus, I had a fairly good idea of what I was about when I joined the other candidates in making the promises. Do we perhaps exert too much pressure on young people to be confirmed when they are not sure if they have the desire? There is a growing trend towards the idea of allowing children of junior age to be confirmed and receive Communion so that they feel part of the Family of Faith with a view to their making a firm decision to follow the Lord Jesus at a mature age. This is fine in theory. As an educationist, I am convinced that the child needs to be nurtured in the Faith through Word *and* Sacrament from an age of discernment such as eight years – which, as teachers will bear witness, is the time at which the average child begins to acquire a keen intellectual and emotional response to the world around them. But will those children be of a mind to make a whole hearted personal commitment to be Christ's faithful soldiers and servants later on? We can only pray that they do. The need to have a more committed Body of Christ is surely not a reflection of "churchmanship" but essential for a Church daring to venture in Mission to the world of the twenty-first century.

Ron would have made a fine priest of the Church. He applied for consideration, with the support of the Vicar of the parish, but, unfortunately, was refused, partly on the basis of a slight stammer in his speech, if you please! His work later took him and Gwyneth to Essex in the 1960's. Sadly he died with much of his life still before him.

As soon as I was confirmed I was asked to take a Sunday school class. They were a class of six year olds, who taught me more than I taught them! One Sunday after Christmas we were dealing with the story of the Flight into Egypt. After the story was read and elaborated upon, the children settled to draw the scene of Joseph leading the donkey, with Mary and baby Jesus on its back.

"It's a fine drawing," I remarked sweetly to one of the girls, *"but what exactly is this strange mark on the donkey's head?"*

"Oh!" said she intrepidly, *"It's what you read to us from the Bible."*

Now more intrigued than ever I said, *"Tell me more, Susan."*

"Well" she continued, unabashed, *"You told us that Joseph did arise with Mary and Jesus and the donkey and flee into Egypt. Here's the flea on the donkey's head!"*

As that old chorus puts it, *"Be careful, little lips, what you say"*. This was one of many instances which formed part of one's "learning curve."

As an illustration of the spirit of commitment that guided Gran's Mill Field days, in winter we used to have to take coal and sticks from home on the bus so that the building had adequate heating. Gran treated all the children as her own, teaching them action songs, bringing every child a small "goody" for singing and listening so well. Bribery? Perhaps so, but all out of love!

Mill Field's days came to an end when I was in my late teens. It had fulfilled its mission to the caravans and an era had finished its course but not before I had preached my first sermon within its walls at the age of seventeen (with the approval of the vicar!). My text was "The Lord is my shepherd, I shall not want". Well, I did not want for a more sure foundation for my spiritual development than the years I spent at Mill Field.

While these years were nurturing me in the Faith, my years as a pupil at Pontypridd Boys' Grammar school were helping to mould my mind. The school commanded a superb view over the town at Coed y Lan and down the valley towards Cardiff. This was significant because during times of day dreaming (which were not a few!) or pretending to think deeply about the "Joymetry" lesson, as our Maths teacher loved to call it, we could look out of the window and be rather more inspired by the landscape and the varying cloud formation. One St. David's Day I recall great excitement as we saw the snowflakes getting larger and larger and, consequently, our enjoyment of the half-day holiday that afternoon getting more and more attractive. Thank God for Dewi Sant!

We were fortunate in having a very well qualified staff, among them some formidable characters. There was, for example, William Lewis, the deputy head who taught Welsh, whom we nicknamed "Willie Woodbine". He was a chapel deacon with a wicked sense of humour, (not always incompatible!) There was "Spitto" Evans, who taught Geography; it was always unwise to sit too near the front in his lessons without the aid of an umbrella! Morien Morgan taught French. He had fought in the Spanish Civil War and had lost an eye for his pains. Morien was married to the well-known T.V. playwright and novelist Elaine Morgan. Our Latin teacher was the Revd. Norman Miles. He was an

Anglican priest who had taken up teaching. His lessons were littered with insights into Church History and Christian teaching in between the parsing of verbs and the exploits of the Roman army in "Caesar's Gallic War".

I soon found that my "forte" was in the Arts rather than the Sciences, as the curriculum was then divided. Words and ideas came to me more easily than numbers and equations. This is why I chose to study Spanish rather than Chemistry and History rather than Physics. However much I deserved to be castigated for my inadequacies in Algebra, one comment on a school report comes to mind for its sheer effrontery. The comment read thus:- *"This pupil has reached rock bottom and is boring through hard"* If these words were intended to shame me into action they failed in their aim because I became an even bigger source of inconvenience to this teacher, for whom I was evidently such a trial. Of course today no teacher could get away with such scornful judgment. There was an unfortunate tendency among some teachers at grammar school level to divide students into "high flyers" and "no hopers". Thus the "no hopers" were often short changed when it came to encouraging them to do better. At least our Woodwork master, "Chippie" Jones, had a more realistic approach. After I had spent a whole term trying to plane a piece of wood twelve inches by four inches for correct alignment without success ("true" was the technical term), he suggested wisely that I throw in the towel and do some extra French during his lessons. What a sensible chap!

One of the "high spots" for me during my school career was to win third prize in a U.K. schools' competition in Spanish. We had to write a Free Composition in that language on the theme of a holiday in Spain. I was in my "O" Level Year at the time. For me the worst part of this achievement was having to be called out to receive the congratulations of the head teacher on the school stage in front of all the pupils. I hated the idea of being singled out, even for something commendable. However I was gratified that my efforts had helped put my school "on the map", especially for the sake of our brilliant Spanish teacher, Jim Young, who spoke about eight languages, including Scottish Gaelic (He was a Scot by birth). It was assumed that, because I was good at Welsh (all of us were learning it as a second language, except for a few boys from Ynysybwl, (a village a few miles north of Pontypridd) that I would be at ease reciting a poem in Welsh at the school Eisteddfod. I failed miserably to make any impression. At least this calamity served to put all further ideas about "putting me on the stage" to rest!

We were most fortunate in having in Mr P. Raymond Jones a head teacher who was a staunch Christian and had that rare gift for commanding not only respect but a certain admiration. His assemblies were top-rate. His short homilies had moral substance and an appeal to integrity that gave us a platform for living as well as learning. One of the ideas he introduced was to invite local clergy and lay people of all denominations to give us a "pep talk". By contrast, in many secondary schools today, assembly consists of a string of school notices and reports of school events with no spiritual and little moral content. For me, listening to those who represented a range of experiences and provided different "slants" on the acting out of the Gospel, did much to develop an openness towards a wider Christian dimension than the one I had hitherto experienced. I remember that it encouraged me to frequent various Christian traditions foreign to me at the time, such as The Pentecostal church and a Quaker Meeting House. To diversify experience is, after all, to be enriched and often leads to returning to your "home territory" the more assured of your convictions.

Here is a simple illustration of the principles upon which the school was based. Raymond Jones was reporting on Monday morning on the previous Saturday's school rugby match. Showering praise on our team he said, *"You may have lost the game, boys, but you did the school proud!"* In those days success did not hinge entirely on the result of the game but the way it was played. Have we gone overboard today in our obsession with winning the biggest prize and undermining the sheer participation? One of my most enjoyable winter pastimes was cross-country running over the hills behind the school, but this was strictly non-competitive! It was great fun and the delight of the warm shower afterwards to get rid of the mud we had gathered on the way was just "fab!"

It was some twenty five years after I left school that I met Raymond Jones at a funeral for a former member of staff who had been a church warden at Aberdare. Typically he greeted me with the welcoming words, *"How good to see you, my boy!"* (I was forty three at the time.) Here was a thorough professional who saw his role as head teacher as primarily a pastoral one. In these days of emphasis in school life and church life, on structure and efficient management, are we in danger of placing the priority of pastoral care and warm relationships on the back burner? Two regrets haunted me on leaving the grammar school to pursue a career at university with eyes firmly fixed on the study of languages. Because we did Latin we were denied a place on the timetable for R.I. (Religious Instruction as it was then called) and Music Appreciation. These two subjects interested me greatly but I was not destined to gain any qualifications in them. However I made up for this later in life through sheer necessity.

My grammar school days were happy days except for compulsory Gymnasium, which I thoroughly detested. The wall bars might just as well have been prison bars! Despite this, I enjoyed Games, even if I did not excel in them. I was happiest with one or two friends rather than a host of them. My best friend was a boy of Italian parents who kept one of several Italian cafes in town – Bruno Marenghi. Other boys called us the Terrible Twins - Meats and Marenghi. We are still in touch today though the miles separate us. It is through Bruno and his family that I came in direct contact with Roman Catholic faith and practice, which again widened my spiritual horizon for what was to come.

I have no regrets about the quality of teaching or the guidance I received at my school together with the friendships shared. One event took place as a premonition of things to come for me. As Form 6 prefects, we were obliged to follow a rota of choosing and reading a passage from the Bible in Assembly, though advice was given if required. I remember choosing the First letter to the Corinthians Chapter Thirteen, the one about Love transcending all virtues. After the assembly one of the Mathematics teachers, who had never taught me and, if he had, would have wished he had not, came up and patted me on the shoulder and said, *"That was an excellent choice of yours and I have never heard it read better. Well done."* To this day I believe that this encouraging comment marked a step towards my ultimate goal in life, if only that teacher had known it at the time. What a difference it makes that praise rather than criticism comes your way especially when it arrives "impromptu"! On reflection, what could be a better platform for the future of any student at a grammar school than to have a staff led by a convinced Christian that also included a priest, a church warden and many dedicated teachers. Some people *know* they have been truly blessed in such influences being freely available.

CHAPTER 3

THE BLACKBOARD YEARS

It had always been a secret ambition of mine to be a teacher ever since I was old enough to think about what I would do with my life. As a lad of about twelve I recall gathering a few younger children together and playing at being in school. Nobody had the audacity to question who would be "in charge" in our role play. But then, the world of "make believe" is natural to children.

Bishop of Llandaff school, Llandaff, Cardiff
(My first teaching post)

I went to Cardiff University. In retrospect I think I might have preferred the more intimate community atmosphere of a place like Aberystwyth but that is "water under the bridge" now. In my first year at Cardiff I studied Welsh, French and Spanish, the latter called, rather pompously, Hispanic Studies. I was minded to specialise in Spanish eventually. However I found the Spanish course rather "hard going"; the medieval poetry which we had to grapple with did not appeal to me very much, so I proceeded in my second year to an Honours Degree course in Welsh. At that time all Degree examinations in Welsh were through the medium of Welsh, whether Welsh was your second or first language. (Since then, Welsh learners are now offered a more modified course) All lectures on Welsh language and literature were in Welsh with no allowance made for those whose "in depth" vocabulary was not as wide as those students who had Welsh from birth. So it was a case of "sink or swim". For the two of us whose first language was English, an introduction to lectures delivered by a native of the Llŷn Peninsular in North Wales was something of a "rough baptism!" We had the considerable task of digesting the content of the lecture (medieval poetry was not that straightforward!) and at the same time getting our ears around the strange sounds that this man was emitting! To be fair, the lecturer may have found the sounds common to us from South Wales strange to his ears!

One of the pleasant outlets for fellowship at Cardiff was gathering as students at the Anglican Chaplaincy, presided over by the fatherly presence of the Revd. Bruce Davies. It was Fr. Bruce who once came as a guest preacher to a service in my home parish. These were the days when you had about a hundred present to welcome a guest preacher on the Sunday evenings in Lent. He was speaking about the "still, small voice" that the prophet Elijah heard on Mount Horeb midst the wind and tempest. As he reached the climax of his theme, lo and behold, the church rang out to the loud clap of thunder and the air was pierced by flashes of lightning. Elijah had come to Pontypridd! Never had I experienced such a positive response to words from the pulpit. Even the normally placid temperament of Fr. Bruce was roused to a mixture of disbelief and natural humour!

Having obtained my degree in 1962 I went on to the Post-Graduate Certificate in Education or Teachers' Training course. I cannot say that I found the tutorials that inspiring but the practical work in the schools was great stuff! I do recall one of the first things that one of the tutors told us at the start of our year's Teachers Training. This was his advice:-

"Ladies and gentlemen, you arrive here, armed with a deep knowledge of your subjects. Your task now is to know John and Mary." Sound instruction for any "know-alls" among us! The point is - the amount of academic knowledge that one possesses does not of itself equip one for competence as a classroom practitioner.

All trainee teachers had to undertake three weeks' practice in a primary school even though their intention was to work, as mine was, at secondary level. I had the privilege of observing classroom activity among Year Five pupils and then give a few lessons under supervision. This age-group is just about the most enthusiastic and creative of all to teach and is especially engaging for "rookies" eager to grasp the necessary "tools of the trade". The imagination that fires the minds of this age-group is so rich and fertile that a "would be" teacher worth his salt is carried along with the flow. I recall a composition being set the class on the theme of *"I am an old oak tree."* One of the children entered into the spirit of life in the forest with a vengeance by admitting, *"I don't like winter very much myself, because Jack Frost comes up behind me and bites my trunk."* You feel like making the comment, *"Naughty Jack Frost!"* I wonder – would this have been the first time that a case of Grievous Bodily Harm had been reported to me? If so, I am afraid I did not report the matter to the police!

The secondary school in which I gained my practice was a recently opened Welsh-medium school, Ysgol Gymraeg Rhydfelen. This school conducted every subject, except English itself, of course, in Welsh. My two subjects were Welsh and French. As at university, being a Welsh learner myself, I had to make sure that my skills in communicating through the medium of Welsh were "au fait" with these students of eleven to sixteen. Try teaching French through Welsh when your natural inclination is to think in English! I was destined to heed the Apostle Paul's words to the Christians at Rome: *"Suffering trains us to endure."*

I was most fortunate to have as my mentor the dynamic Miss Nia Daniel, who together with her sister Ethne, did so much for the Welsh Language cause in the Cardiff area where they lived. She was so sympathetic and patient with me as well as tremendously keen to encourage any potential she may have detected in me. One of her personal observations stands out in my memory. Once, when we were sharing some reflections on how my lesson had gone, she remarked. *"Alan, you have a very classical mind."* I was not sure whether this was good or bad news! I suppose it was neither, just stating a fact of life! So all my mental inadequacies can be laid at the door of a classical mind! The college tutor, J. B. Davies, summarised my achievements at the end of the year's training by remarking that *"His efforts to communicate relevantly with pupils may be somewhat blunted by his natural diffidence"*, in other words, my tendency to shyness and self-effacement may be a stumbling block on the path to success as a teacher. So I had to learn to be more assertive in order to gain pupils' attention! At the end of the day I obtained my Diploma with merit. The learning process had started.

Meanwhile I was now twenty three years of age and had been accepted for training as a Reader within the Church in Wales, which was the minimum age to be licensed to this ministry. Those who have embarked on a Readers' course will know that it is no "walk-over". There were three examinations to sit – Biblical Studies, Worship and Doctrine with an oral test in taking a service and preaching a sermon. We were instructed to preach for no more than *eight* minutes! Regular preachers on Sunday, please note! Thus it happened that the year that I became a qualified teacher coincided with being a licensed Reader of the Church. These two passions in my life were already running along parallel lines. During the next six years I was to function often on Sundays not only in my home parish but also in churches throughout the Rhondda Deanery where there happened to be the need for "cover" for a priest who was ill, on holiday or else where a parish was vacant. So for those years I was employed as a school teacher in the week and doing voluntary work at week-ends. Not quite moonlighting! I was later to find that the one activity complimented the other rather than detracted from it.

Meanwhile, my first teaching post found me at the newly built Bishop of Llandaff Church in Wales High School. It was opened in October 1963 by H.R.H. Princess Margaret and her husband, Lord Snowdon. Each member of staff was stationed at strategic points in the school for the Royal Tour of the building after the official opening ceremony. I was in the Library. I was impressed by the wealth of interest shown by Lord Snowdon in Welsh culture and history. I should have realised that, as Anthony Armstrong-Jones, he had a strong Welsh background. One can always draw on one's roots!

The fact that we were only ten full-time staff serving some four hundred pupils at that time meant that most staff had to teach an alternative subject to complete the timetable. The head teacher needed to be released from classroom duties for two terms to concentrate on his administrative work. So the lot fell on me to take a Year Seven class in Geography. Not my favourite subject in school by any means! On the understanding that we would concentrate on Wales and the rest of the U.K. I endured those two terms. I think I worked harder than any of my pupils to prepare lessons in order to keep one step ahead all the time. The ratio of staff to pupils also meant that, as staff, we were only one day a week free from supervision duty in the school yard, at lunch time and conducting "detention" after school. These were the days when there were no dinner ladies or playground supervisers. All this taught me how to adapt and take what comes.

As one responsible for the teaching of Welsh, I felt bound to set up a school branch of Urdd Gobaith Cymru, the Young People's Movement in Wales. This League of Activity is unique to Wales and encourages much interest among young people in learning Welsh through a wide range of activities, including sport and summer camps. Its triple motto, displayed on its triangular badge of Red, White and Green, stands for three loyalties which sit well in a church school setting, namely, Loyalty to Wales, Loyalty to Christ and Loyalty to One Another. Being attached to this movement involved competitions in drama, recitation, singing and games at local, county and national levels. Although this involvement was quite time-consuming, sometimes extending to Saturdays as well as after the school day, it was an opportunity for me to "tap into" children's interests and skills beyond the classroom routine. It opened the door to social contact which time spent in the classroom did not allow – to refer back to my college tutor's words, "to get to know *all* about John and Mary!" On two occasions I spent a week at Llangrannog Summer Camp as a leader/official, which was great fun. In that Spartan era boys were accommodated in tents and girls in huts (in those days the "gentler sex" had special treatment, notice!). Nowadays they all have en-suite accommodation and a ski-slope for good measure! After helping to wash up about four hundred cups, saucers, plates and dishes after each meal. I think the modern dishwasher would be a "walkover!"

On Sunday mornings I marched our eighteen pupils to the village church which had the effect of making their school status stand out among all the "campers."

The second year at the school saw a big increase in the number of Pupils on Roll and a consequent increase in staff. A new French graduate came to oversee the French department, leaving me with just a few lessons in that subject. That year we took twenty six pupils to Brittany where the native Breton language is closely linked to Welsh, despite the predominance of French. So this educational holiday neatly blended the twin interests of Welsh and French studies,

With the co-operation of the Head of Religious Education I planned a bilingual form of service for school assembly. This development helped to give the Welsh language a boost in status as a medium of communication in School Worship and not simply limited to a subject on the curriculum. Seeds were definitely being sown here for the future ministry in which I would be involved.

Pupils of Bishop of Llandaff High School were drawn from a large area of the Cardiff area and from a variety of backgrounds. There were children from the Docks and Splott areas of white and West Indian ethnic origins, together with former pupils of Llandaff City Primary School, most of whom came from affluent families. Here again the challenge to be adaptable and to be able to communicate with pupils of different levels of intelligence and different cultural situations came into play.

The Head Teacher of the school was Michael Roberts, himself the son of a clergyman. Michael was an urbane, kindly and approachable person. He played a prominent part in the life of the community in

Whitchurch, Cardiff, being a local councillor and Justice of the Peace. A few years after I left the school he became an M.P. and served as parliamentary secretary of state in the Heath administration. Sadly he died in office with an aspiring political future ahead of him. The staff were a happy blend of youth and experience. I was fortunate to have such a closely-knit group of colleagues in which to grow in confidence and share experiences for good or ill.

It was during the first year at the school that I met and forged a friendship with Sheila Govett who had come to complete her final year as student teacher at Cyncoed Teachers' College, specialising in Music, R.E. and English. Her surname "Spurgeon-Govett" displayed a little of her ancestry, since on her father's side the family was linked to the famous Baptist preacher, Charles Haddon Spurgeon, who founded the Spurgeon Bible College in London. Sheila was the organist and musical director at St. John the Baptist church in Sully, near Barry and also a Guide and Brownie leader in the village. After her college training was completed she obtained a teaching post at Llanrumney High school, on the eastern edge of Cardiff. We managed to see each other only as commitments allowed, unfortunately. We found that we had much in common. Most weeks, Saturday was the only option open to us for meeting up in term time. However they say that "absence makes the heart grow fonder!"

In 1966 I decided that I needed to "move on" in order to extend my teaching range to some Form Six work and so took up the post of Welsh teacher with some R.E. at Aberdare Boys' Grammar school at the top of the Cynon valley. Here was a distinctive "valleys" community familiar to me, but somewhat more markedly Welsh in identity than that of my upbringing. Whereas in the school at Cardiff there had not been a single pupil from a Welsh-speaking background, here a number of boys were fairly fluent in Welsh. The opportunity of assisting with R.E. (despite my lack of paper qualifications in this subject) provided a welcome variety from teaching a language. Here was scope to identify with a "whole-child" approach towards a pupil. Here was the need to explore in relevant terms for the pupil the meaning of life, the value of personal relationships as well as making the Bible and Christian traditions relevant to them. The Head of R.E. was a Non-conformist minister, the Revd. Ivor Parry. He had written an acclaimed book in Welsh on the nature and history of Non-conformity in Wales which deserved to be translated into English so as to be available to a wider readership. Ivor was a very perceptive, witty individual, a good conversationalist and "raconteur" of stories. We got on splendidly and had a mutual respect for each other's different Christian traditions. It is true to say that we were both open-minded about the differing interpretations of teaching and practice that might place many Christians at loggerheads with each other.

In this all-male staff room (we had a female school secretary and one female member of the school laboratory), serious discussions of issues of the day (no party politics, please!) jostled with riotous laughter as we shared views and news. For much of the time conversation was in Welsh. I well remember that horrendous day when slurry from a coal tip engulfed the junior school at Aberfan. Our school was located just over the mountain from Aberfan, but you had to travel down one valley and up another to get there. The strange thing was that on that particular October morning I travelled to school from my home in Pontypridd a different way. Having left my brief case at my aunt's house in the Rhondda the evening before, I needed to collect it on the way to school. I arrived a few minutes late to hear in the staff room that a major incident had occurred in the former mining village of Aberfan in the Merthyr valley. Several of the Form 6 students acted as volunteers in the rescue operation. The scenes of horror left an indelible mark on them. The then Vicar of Aberfan, whose brother was a chorister in my home parish, had a nervous breakdown as a result of the tragedy from which he never recovered and tragically died some three years later.

I continued my work with the Urdd at the school, assisting the Head of Department. I remember taking some pupils to the National Urdd Eisteddfod at Holyhead. They collected second prize, to the acclaim of the Head Teacher and boys.

I have to say that it was a refreshing change to share the teaching of Welsh with students of Form 6. I am one of those who feels that a secondary/comprehensive school that has no Form 6 (Advanced Level students) is something like a regiment whose officers are missing. The Senior Form offers the rest of the school a kind of pattern for adult life to which to aspire. By its prefect system it sets down markers for behaviour, while supporting staff in the need to encourage a sense of responsibility and accountability. Many who enter the many tertiary colleges of today at sixteen are not ready for the individual study and self-discipline required of them. They have not reached the stage of academic rigour which comes when they begin their courses at Further or Higher Education. This is just a personal opinion of course but a firmly held one. As it was, I shared enthusiastically with small groups of students aged sixteen to eighteen insights into literature in a more relaxed and mature atmosphere than is possible in a class of thirty or more younger pupils.

After being in the school about two terms I decided to form, with the approval of the head teacher (who happened to be an Anglican), an after-school Christian Guild which was open to those of the Christian faith, any other faith (we had two Jehovah Witnesses and one Hindu) and those who professed no particular faith. I confess that I wondered whether this step might be a bit of a "shot in the dark" but in fact it attracted an attendance of about twenty five or so boys every month. We held quizzes, "Any Questions?" sessions and guest speakers to share their experiences etc. We had lively discussions on moral issues, including the relevance of institutional religion, comparing and contrasting Life with Jesus and Life within the Church. One of the speakers whom I invited to come and speak to us was the son of the former vicar of Pontypridd, the Revd. David Richards, who, like his father before him, had worked as a missionary for some time. With the setting up of this Guild a new boundary had been reached, namely, the discovery of what was important about life in the minds of the pupils. In classroom routine the question "How?" seems to be all important. Now the question "Why?" assumed as much, if not, more importance. It is in the exploring of "Why?" that young people develop morally and spiritually.

At Easter 1968 the Head of the Welsh department was appointed to a headship in Carmarthen and I was appointed to succeed him. It was in September of that year that I came to a decision with which I had been wrestling for some time. I was becoming more and more involved with life in the Church. In 1967 I had been elected to represent my home parish at the meetings of the Governing Body of the Church in Wales. This was the period when important discussions were taking place about plans to unite the Church with the Wesleyan Methodist Church, or, should I say, to welcome that Church back into the fold of the Anglican Church from which it broke away in the eighteenth century with the ministry of John Wesley, who was an ordained Anglican.

I found these debates very intriguing from the theological point of view. The net result was to encourage me to "search my soul" for conclusions and reach not only conclusions, but also firmer convictions. At last I came to a firm decision – that God was calling me to serve Him in the ordained ministry. I went to see the Head Teacher, Mr Jess Warren, rather nervously, expecting perhaps a dismissive response to my personal decision. Much to my astonishment and relief, his reply was, *"Congratulations! I am not in the least surprised! I wish you well!"*

So after two terms as Head of Department I was not only leaving Aberdare Boys' Grammar School but turning my back on the blackboard and the staff room.

To this day I have never regretted those years in front of a class which preceded my being accepted for ordination. They had given me a wealth of experience of relating to students of a wide age range and of working alongside and in harmony with colleagues as a team of professional people. I think that my period of teaching was a sound basis on which to build a ministry of proclaiming my faith and enabling others to proclaim theirs. Year by year during those years in school the ripple on the pond was spreading ever more widely as "knowledge of subject" progressed to "knowledge of John and Mary". Communicating subject material in the classroom would become communicating the Faith in a parish setting, but people and their needs and problems would be the context from now on.

Perhaps the farewell occasion at the end of that last school term is worth recording. I had been invited to give a short homily in the school's Christmas Carol Service the week before. My theme had been that of the significance of the coming of Christ into the world at Bethlehem. I described His coming into the world as an exercise in making contact with us as human beings. I said, *"Boys, would you expect a rugby coach to turn up at your training session dressed in a bowler hat and carrying an umbrella?"* I waited for the laughter to subside. *"I thought you wouldn't. No, you would expect him to put on a track suit and be alongside the team in training. Only in this way would he be respected and only thus would he be able to get his message across to them and so help them deliver the goods. Well, this is what Christians believe about why Jesus came into the world. The team was playing badly and they needed a pep-talk from the head coach! To fulfil this aim he had to come down to our level in order to get the best out of us!"*

At the last school assembly three members of staff happened to be leaving. I was glad I did not stick out like a sore thumb on my own! I responded to the good wishes expressed on my behalf by giving the boys of the school a parting piece of advice. *"However committed you may be (and I hope you all are) to achieving good qualifications in school and thereafter in your careers, it is the quality of your characters that will be your greatest asset on life's journey. What you do and how you succeed is vitally important, but what is of even more lasting importance is "What you are as a person in relation to others."*

It was this sentiment that coloured the step I was about to take, namely, to abandon the corridor and the classroom in favour of the altar and the pulpit. It would also involve a change of uniform!

CHAPTER 4

LEARNING THE CLERICAL TRADE

How times have changed since the late 1960's when I was accepted for ordination training. Now there are Residential Selection Courses with Selections Panels helping the Diocesan Bishop to decide on the suitability

St. Catherine's church, Pontypridd

of each candidate for ordination. In my time, it was simply an interview with the Warden of Ordinands and, if at this initial meeting one was approved, a meeting with the bishop at the end of which you were informed if you had been accepted. In my case it so happened that I had taught the son of the Warden of Ordinands while at Bishop of Llandaff High School, so we had met each other in the roles of parent and teacher. When the then Archbishop of Wales, Glyn Simon, interviewed me, I recall him telling me that there were three aspects to the sacred ministry to be borne in mind – the spiritual aspect, the teaching aspect and the pastoral aspect. He asked me to single out which one of these was most crucial to my way of thinking. Perhaps, given my background, he would have expected me to choose the teaching aspect. However, I told him that, for me, unless we care pastorally for those we are called to serve then all other aspects serve little purpose; in other words, our prayer life, our preaching, our entire role as priests must be driven by a deep-seated care and concern for the spiritual well-being of others. I am convinced that my teaching experience and my years as a Licensed Reader hitherto helped me to strike a convincing note (hopefully) and not sound as though I had lifted my thoughts from a text-book that I had read.

When I entered St. Michael's Theological College at the age of 28 there were only two ordinands older than myself. One was Harry Dudley, aged 55, and a former employee at a printing works. For our sins Harry and I were put in charge of the annual publication of the College Magazine, Harry for his experience in the field of printing and me because I had not yet acquired the gift of saying "No!" At least the work of collating suitable articles for inclusion in the publication prepared the way for that chore of all chores for clergy, the Parish Magazine! Harry and I became great friends through working in harness with this project and I was honoured to be his first Harvest guest preacher when he entered his first parish of Cwmcarn, near Cross Keys. The other students at St. Michael's were all in their early 20's, some pursuing Degree and Diploma courses in Theology or Divinity, while several slighter older ones had come from other theological colleges to complete their training by doing a year of Pastoral Studies with us. In my time of course we were *male* ordinands only. A few were married and lived with their wives on the college site. Today of course our theological colleges embrace both genders and most students arrive having been engaged in other spheres of employment for many years.

I found it a very traumatic experience being "relegated" from the heights of a Head of Department in a staff room of my own to being a student behind a desk in a lecture room, sitting at the feet of teachers. Again adaptability was called for together with a dose of openness to receive new insights. The year before training I had begun the London University Bachelor of Divinity Degree course so the Warden of the college allowed me to continue with that course and attend only the General Ordination compulsory lectures in Ethics, Anglican Doctrine and Worship. The result of this arrangement was that I completed my training in less than two years, being made deacon in Llandaff Cathedral on the Feast of St. James in July 1970 and priested there on the Feast of the Transfiguration in August 1971.

With my hand on my heart, I cannot say that I found my theological training terribly exciting, perhaps because I had been conducting public services for several years and was already well into my External Divinity Course. It was more a natural progression rather than a steep, learning curve. The most rewarding aspect was the fellowship of other students and a close relationship with the four staff members with whom we shared three meals daily as well as two or even three daily college chapel services (counting Compline held on three evenings) as well as the lectures. Some lectures were at the University where we were joined by students of the Cardiff Baptist College, others were at St. Michael's. There were four members of staff- Chancellor Geoffrey Rees, Warden, Revd.Cledan Mears, Sub-Warden, (later Bishop of Bangor), Revd. Michael Bowles (Chaplain and New Testament Studies) and Fr. Colin Sykes (Old Testament Studies and Philosophy).

The Warden lectured to us on Church History and the Sub-Warden lectured to us in Doctrine. I had always found the Doctrine of the Trinity a bit if a mountain to climb. I think this is true of most students of theology. We had four lectures exploring the history of this doctrine and the way it had been a subject of controversy among Christians through the ages. Despite the high standard of teaching on Cledan Mears' part and the intriguing ideas that we shared, I was no wiser at the end of the course of lectures than at the start! Imagine my relief when Cledan, sensing this reaction to be fairly common among his students, reassured us by saying, *"We are not meant to understand the Trinity as a concept, only to accept it, through our experience, as being true."* Is this where, once again, the intellect fails and where faith takes over?

One other incident has stayed with me. Michael Bowles was discussing with us the comparative virtues of various commentaries on St. Luke's Gospel. He explained, *Commentary A has the greatest depth of scholarship, Commentary B gives us the most informed background information but Commentary C is the most inspiring. This is why, gentlemen, I would recommend for your studies Commentary C.* I remember these words so well simply because later in life I have come to value the maxim that unless our people are *inspired* by what we share with them of the Gospel, no amount of instruction or scholarship, however profound and well-intentioned, will impact upon them for good.

Two amusing stories are worth relating. I was on serving duty one Friday morning when the Warden was celebrating the Eucharist. The service began at 7.30 a.m. in college chapel. Unfortunately I forgot to set my alarm and I woke up with a start to find that my clock read 7.15 a.m. I had the quickest wash ever and decided that my cassock over my pyjamas would save me losing more time in dressing. I sprinted in rather undignified style to the vestry. Struggling to recover my breath I gasped, *"Good morning, Father"*. Glancing at me from top to toe, Geoffrey Rees, with that sardonic humour of his, observed, *"Alan, I thought the liturgical colour for Lent was purple, but I notice* (pointing to my pyjama bottoms which were sticking out at the bottom of my cassock) *that you have mistaken purple for blue."* Despite my embarrassment I had the presence of mind to quip, *"Sorry, Father, I have a habit of getting into hot water with liturgical niceties."* He was gracious enough to smile at this admission. I had the distinct impression however that the Absolution after the Confession was pronounced more robustly than usual that morning!

Another slightly more embarrassing chapel occasion for me involved serving at the altar for Fr. Sykes. This was the weekly 1662 Prayer Book Communion service – one that I, being of a slightly older age-group than most students, was nurtured on as a youngster. In this Rite the ablutions are completed at the very end of the service. However, Fr. Sykes, true to the recently introduced Experimental Rite of the Church in Wales of the 1960's, offered the chalice to me for the start of the ablutions after the Communion was completed and not at the very end. I firmly stood my ground but with my conscience intact while Fr. Sykes saw to the ablutions himself. In the vestry afterwards he asked me politely what the game was! I equally politely countered, *"I'm sorry, Father, but I presumed that if we are doing the 1662 Service, we are doing it all by the book or not at all."* He did not appear to be totally convinced! No grudge was borne by either of us after this incident, naturally, but for some reason I cannot recall being on the rota to serve for Fr. Sykes after this! Another lesson for life – we can beg to differ, but we can stay friends. Sadly Colin died while serving as Vicar of Abergavenny in middle age – a sad loss to the Church.

I have to admit that, as someone trained to make sure that there was always an emphasis on communicating in a "down-to-earth" manner, as close to children's experience as possible, the lectures on Philosophy of Religion, smacked of an alien tongue. I much preferred to grapple with the actual text of a Pauline letter in front of me, word for word, than theorise, however entertainingly, about the insights of Don Cupitt or Bultmann. Truth to tell, I am more enthusiastic about Applied Theology than Pure Theology. Is it because the latter is mentally engaging in that it promotes depth of thought whereas the former is dynamic and provides motivation for giving practical expression to our faith?

As students we went for practice in conducting services to churches in the immediate area – some in the Vale of Glamorgan, some in the valleys, while many Welsh-speaking ordinands like myself had to function in Dewi Sant Church, the former St. Andrew's, in the centre of Cardiff which provides services in Welsh only. The vicar of Dewi Sant at that time was the Revd. George Noakes, who was to become the Archbishop of Wales. I little dreamt that within 20 years Archbishop George would be offering me a parish in the "foreign" diocese of St. Davids! So the only sermons in training college that I ever preached were in Welsh! I suppose that even then the writing was on the wall that wherever I would travel in ministry, the Welsh language would not be far behind!

One highlight of my theological training came at the very end when the Warden informed me that I had been awarded the Archdeacon Lawrence Thomas Memorial Prize, which enabled me to purchase books of my choice to the amount of £100. There was however a sting in the tail. I had to preach in Archdeacon Thomas's former parish church of Holy Trinity, Aberafan, near Port Talbot. Gran and my god-mother (who were two great friends and had naturally followed my career with interest) came with me for moral support.

Sheila and I were engaged during the last three months of my time in St. Michael's and were married on

Easter Monday, April 12th. 1971 at Sully Parish church, eight months into my curacy in Pontypridd. The Rector of Sully, the Revd. Basil Jones, performed the ceremony, assisted by my vicar, Canon Vernon Payne. Basil insisted playfully that, as I was taking away his organist and choir mistress, that I should pay him a transfer fee! You can imagine that, after the hectic period of Holy Week and Easter Sunday, neither of us was exactly as fresh as a daisy for the day itself! With the brownies, guides and large choir present to represent Sheila's local activities, there was just about room in the church for families and friends. Our honeymoon was spent in the Cotswolds.

I was to serve my title as assistant curate of my home parish of Pontypridd, Saint Catherine, However I was not to turn my back entirely on St. Michael's College because during my first year as priest I was invited by the Warden to take optional oral classes in the use of Welsh for students and any staff who wished to attend. Among my "pupils" were the Revd. David Thomas who later became Provincial Assistant Bishop and whose father Bishop J.J. Thomas was to induct me to my first incumbency, also Robert Williams, later to become Archdeacon of Gower, and my good friend, Malcolm Davies, a native of Llanelli, who, although a fluent Welsh speaker himself, was kind enough to give me moral support in the promotion of confidence among the learners. I enjoyed this return to teaching in relaxed mode on a voluntary basis. We had lots of fun and I felt I was providing a basis for these students to pursue speaking Welsh in the parishes in which they would possibly serve.

It was indeed most unusual for a deacon to start out in the parish that nurtured him, but as I had been allowed to do some pastoral work one afternoon a week in the parish with some success while at St. Michael's, Archbishop Glyn thought that it would be good to build on that ground work, as long as I had no qualms, which I did not. It was a slight gamble in the sense that parishioners could be too familiar with the Alan that had grown up among them and therefore perhaps less respectful of my efforts in the role of the curate with the collar worn back to front. Fears of this kind were ill founded. People were tremendously supportive and took no unfair liberties whatsoever. Besides which, the bulk of my efforts were to be directed towards a large housing estate at Glyncoch, located between Pontypridd and Ynysybwl with its modern, dual-purpose church of All Saints, dating from the early 1960's, an area unfamiliar to me before my contact during college days.

Sheila and I set up home in a dormer bungalow in the White Rock Estate, high above the town of Pontypridd and about three miles from Glyncoch. The bungalow was located, appropriately enough, in "Nun's Crescent", a reference to the name of the local farm, "Gellifynaches" ("Nun's Grove"). I believe that the name refers to some holy well in the vicinity that has since been filled up, either deliberately or unwittingly. This modern bungalow was an ideal place to set up home – small enough to be manageable but with a pleasant and conveniently sized garden to front and back which suited us as lovers of the "outdoors". The only problem was that the soil was heavy with clay, which was fine for growing roses but hopeless for setting up a vegetable plot! Still we made up for this by growing tomatoes, cucumbers and courgettes under cold frames. I know that many clergy claim a deficiency in possessing "green fingers" and despair of maintaining gardens but, as long as the garden is not too large, being busy in the garden can be very therapeutic.

Fortunately, Sheila had managed to get a transfer from the school in Llanrumney to one closer to home at Ferndale in the Rhondda. Thus a stressful journey through part of Cardiff and then up the busy A 470 became a straightforward journey up the Rhondda valley of about 25 minutes. The school, Ferndale Girls' Secondary, was pleasantly situated close to Darren Park, complete with its lake. Sheila taught Music and R.E. and easily made friends on the staff with such as Mary Shotton and Hawys James, wife of Councillor Glyn James. Hawys was well known locally for her Welsh folk songs for young people, both as singer and composer. The redoubtable Mrs Fox (of the Fox Funeral Director family) was the head teacher. She managed the school with a firm but caring hand, the result being, as Sheila found, a harmonious and cohesive atmosphere with regard to staff and pupils. There are those who champion the cause of schools of mixed gender, claiming that the pupils benefit from a natural integration for social and moral development, preparing them in a positive way for adulthood and its personal relationships and responsibilities. I think that this is certainly true of primary schools in which it is desirable that such young children have the advantage of a mixed environment because at this stage they see school life as a natural extension of home life, where siblings are often of the other sex. However the secondary stage can bring more complex problems with pupils going through the adolescent stages of pubity and its emotional repercussions and the growing need to assert the sexual claims of one gender on the other. The result of this can often be a trend towards "bravado" and unwelcome "exhibitionism" that can cause pupils to be detracted from full achievement academically and can undermine school discipline. Both Sheila and I had experienced teaching at a mixed school and a single-sex school and our experience was that, on the whole, life was more straightforward and free from unwarranted tensions in a single-sex school. After all, pupils can still enjoy the company of the other gender outside school hours and schools meet up socially at all kinds of sporting and music events etc. One can only speak of one's own experience. This I will say undeniably about all types of school - much of the distinctive ethos prevailing at the school depends on its management by senior staff and the personality of the head teacher himself/herself.

I had already made contact with the good folk of Ferndale, having been asked as a Reader to take a monthly Welsh service at St. Dunstan's church (surely an exceptional dedication of a church in Wales) since the vicar of the parish could not manage Welsh. Having been ordained priest, The Archdeacon of Margam, the Venerable Eric Roberts, asked me to relieve him of his monthly duty of celebrating the Eucharist there. Thus I had a fortunate introduction to bilingualism in the life of the Church. I continued this monthly Welsh "stint" while I served my title in Pontypridd. In 1973 Archdeacon Roberts was appointed Bishop of St. Davids, and before leaving the Llandaff diocese, he kindly presented me with a red stole on behalf of the congregation as a token of his appreciation of my help at Ferndale. I am still proud to wear that stole today, with its happy memories of the faithful at St. Dunstan's. The mainstay of that little group of faithful worshippers was Professor Evan John Jones, former Professor of Education at Swansea University and a fluent Welshman of the "purist" kind. I and many Welsh-speaking ordinands at St.Michael's College who went to take Evensong there during training have cause to be grateful to Evan John for his encouragement to us, his gems of wisdom, and his presence as a mentor of our sermons. I certainly had to make sure that my soft mutations in Welsh (such a problem sometimes to the casual speaker!) were accurate with an academic of such repute "hanging on your every word". I think that my time at St. Dunstan's was a true extension of my theological training for good.

Meanwhile we were settling in at Nun's Crescent and battling with the clay soil, trusting that the parish work would not be as strenuous! The estate at Glyncoch was situated half way between Pontypridd and Ynysybwl, accommodating about 3,500 souls. Its church of All Saints was built in the early 1960's in the rather fallacious notion during that decade that every new large housing complex needed a church built on it. It would have made more sense, it seems to me, had the Church sought to build a church school rather than a church building, wherever affordable, in such areas. A school would have provided families with a Church focus and enabled the Church to build up a family of Faith within a community that needed a real sense of identity. As it was, churches that sprang up in such nondescript areas struggled for the most part to survive against a background of social deprivation with residents feeling uprooted from their previous established communities.

My first Sunday after I was made a deacon bore witness to the uphill task to come. There were just fourteen communicants to welcome me!

Helped by Sheila's musical abilities we set about encouraging children to take part in the choir and tried building up a Sunday school and Youth Club. More often than not, young people are willing to try something new without the inhibitions of older people and, through their participation, we hoped that parents and friends would "capture the spirit". We were able to enlist the help of teachers and leaders (without whom no progress could be made) and things began to take off! A Ladies Guild was formed to organise fund-raising events and thus create a fellowship group as a potential gateway towards joining us for worship. By its organising efforts this group introduced me to the delights of the Jumble Sale. This name for a Sale of second - hand items is frowned upon now in these more sophisticated times. We refer now to a "Nearly New Sale" or "Second owner products for sale" or else a more genteel "Afternoon Tea with stalls". However in the early 1970's at Glyncoch, Jumble Sales were looked forward to with great eagerness by many who found that, seeking an item at a 60% discount was too much of a temptation to resist. I well remember a very damp Saturday afternoon when, before I rolled up my sleeves for action, I carefully placed my mackintosh on the top of the piano, out of harm's way (as I thought!). When this particular lady brought her many purchases of clothing for payment (I found out later that she made a profession out of selling those items bought at Jumble Sales to market vendors for a considerable profit) I noticed to my horror that *my* mackintosh was among her items. I rushed up to rescue my garment from the heap of clothes she held, saying,

"*I' m sorry, Dorcas, that mac is not for sale*" "*Oh!*" said she, unabashed," *I was only going to offer £5 for it anyway as it looks a bit tatty,*" to which I snapped hotly, "*Thanks, Dorcas, I gave £32 for it last year in Marks and Spencers.*" She parted with the mac rather ungraciously. That Jumble Sale, like all of them, was a huge success financially, helping us to complete the repaying of the outstanding debt on the Building Fund within a year.

We also began a less "frenetic" and more enjoyable activity by holding a monthly Church Hop. This was an informal social event with the accent on dancing, even those with two left feet like me. The leading organisers were the first couple that I married in my ministry – a joy to know that a couple blessed in marriage can follow it up with such a practical role to play in the life of the church.

One of the most difficult situations in ministry is to officiate at the funeral of a child, especially one that you have known well. We had a child, Stephen, in our Sunday school suffering from birth from a form of poliomyelitis. The poor lad had no arms or legs. His parents were told that he would not survive beyond the age of 6. In fact Stephen was a lively member of our Sunday school until the age of 11 when his condition deteriorated rapidly. He was such a lively, cheerful chap whose personality had become very much part of the scene on Sunday. Needless to say, there was hardly a dry eye at his funeral service. A child of that age has developed into a character who is cherished and will never be forgotten. Ministry to a family who has lost a child and ministering to a family whose dear one has taken his or her life are always the most challenging, from a pastoral point of view.

One thing I developed in Glyncoch as time went on was a skill in measuring glass window panes accurately and even getting to replace them myself. Often we would have a spate of vandalism of this kind. Once at Harvest time there was an almighty bang in the entrance porch of the church. A firework had been thrown inside the entrance door. Luckily nobody was in the path of the firework at the time. Such unhappy events are all part of what happened on many of such large housing estates during this period. They did not however daunt our efforts to share the Love of Christ with the many people of good will that resided there.

I had always aimed to provide two over-riding elements in worship – the capacity to be lively and informal (when required) and at the same time to present a sense of dignity and "otherness". In other words, the old maxim of the "horizontal and the vertical" ways of "doing church" in which we combine the human and the divine dimensions. After two years into my time in Glyncoch an interesting experiment was initiated. By now we were getting about an average of forty or so on average Sunday worshippers. The idea offered a new dimension to the outreach of the Church. The suggestion arose out of the fact that a minister representing the United Reformed Church, but who was unable for health reasons to continue with responsibilities for a pastorate, would join me to form an informal ecumenical venture. This involved pastoral collaboration, a Free Service on three Sunday evenings a month and a monthly afternoon informal service based on the format of Evensong in which both he and I participated. All this of course was in addition to the usual weekly Anglican Eucharist on Sunday morning at which I presided. This worked well for three good reasons, (a) the minister concerned, Revd. John Henson, lived on the spot, unlike me, so between us we could arrange visits, meetings etc. to mutual convenience, (b) John was not averse to Anglican liturgy; in fact he had attended a church primary school as a child and (c) it was important in such an experimental situation to keep options open and be prepared to be adaptable and spontaneous. It is amazing what Christians can achieve together when respecting each other's traditions go hand in hand with a dose of flexibility to ensure the widest appeal with the least offence caused. With most housing estates of the 1960's kind there is a mission field scenario in the offing and one must be prepared to take risks and be relevant to the spiritual needs that face you. I have to say that my own ministry as an Anglican priest was enriched by this approach, but more importantly, it provided the worshippers at All Saints an opportunity to widen the horizon of their Christian fellowship through a diversity of worship and tradition

I still treasure the Baptist Hymnal (with full music) that John kindly gave Sheila and me on our leaving Glyncoch. He was a very musically minded person himself.

I make no apology for highlighting my work in Glyncoch to the seeming detriment of the rest of the parish of St. Catherine in which I was the assistant priest, but my vicar, Canon Vernon Payne, had entrusted me with the pastoral responsibility there and I was thus free, with his blessing, to take a lead in this part of the parish. I was responsible for the weekly Youth Fellowship attached to St. Catherine's, which we named "Cymry'r Groes" after the popular youth movement in the 1950's and 1960's. I also acted as Deanery Youth Chaplain for the years during which I was a curate and chaplain to the Pontypridd Air Training Corps. I recall a memorable trip to London's West End when we took 45 teenagers from St. Catherine's and All Saints to see the stage musical "Jesus Christ Superstar". There was an unexpected bonus to this trip. I had arranged for us to have a guided tour of Westminster Abbey. After contacting the senior sacristan at the Abbey I was informed that on that day there was to be a Commonwealth Day Service which her Majesty the Queen and Prince Philip would attend, together with celebrities from the world of the Arts, such as the violinist, Yehudi Menuhin and the actress, Anna Neagle, both of whom read passages of Scripture in the service. Imagine the excitement when, as we were gathered as a group at the west door of the Abbey, the Royals arrived within a few yards of us. Surely those young people would always remember that trip to London and that they went in the name of their church. The musical was an exciting experience too, though I, for one, would have appreciated less volume in the use of the microphones!

Life as a curate was fairly hectic. There wasn't a dull moment. Indeed, with Sheila teaching, we had just Saturday to ourselves. This was not always sacrosanct either because during the winter months the Saturday mornings were sometimes taken up with taking boys from the All Saints Youth club to inter-church soccer matches. In addition to this, on a Saturday there was always the occasional church fete or wedding to attend. Did anyone say that a clergyman works only on a Sunday? Don't you believe it!

One aspect I found very satisfying was to take a service of Holy Communion alternately with the vicar at the Pontypridd Institute for the Deaf and Dumb once a month. It was so satisfying seeing the faces of these people when you gave them the Sacrament and spoke to them afterwards. To have to slow down the speed of the spoken word so that the interpreter could translate for them caused you to think more profoundly about the meaning of what you were saying. We can so easily and unthinkingly "trot out" the familiar words of our liturgy so that significance suffers. It was spiritually enriching for me to be uplifted by their cheerful and welcoming company after the service over refreshments. What a privilege to minister to these needy people. We learn so much from them.

My time in the parish of Saint Catherine's, Pontypridd, was hard–going, as far as All Saints was concerned, but enlightening and most rewarding. I had learned much and had taken a lot of responsibility that would have been denied many serving their title. I was fortunate that I had been given almost a "free hand" to take initiatives and make my mistakes. But another door of ministry was about to open unexpectedly. The ministry I would be leaving behind would be effectively taken up by my successor, The Revd. Bill Thomas, who later became the Archdeacon of Margam. Meanwhile my responsibilities would continue in a different setting altogether.

CHAPTER 5

TASTING LIFE AS A VICAR

After three and a half years in the parish of St. Catherine's, Pontypridd, to my great surprise, and to be honest, my slight dismay, as I felt that my ministry in Glyncoch was really "taking off", the Bishop of Llandaff, Eryl Thomas, invited me to discuss the possibility of my joining a new parish project in the Rhondda. The idea was to set up a Rectorial Benefice with myself as a vicar with pastoral oversight of the previous parish made up

St. Peter's church, Pentre, Rhondda

of Saint Peter's Pentre with the parish church of Ystradyfodwg (St. John Baptist) in Ton Pentre. The then vicar of Ystrad Rhondda would continue to have oversight of his area within the benefice as the other vicar in the team and the then vicar of Ton Pentre, St. David's and St. Mark's, Gelli would continue his oversight there but become the new rector (incumbent) of the benefice. However, by the time I had my interview with Bishop Eryl, the parish of Ystrad Rhondda had withdrawn from the initiative and it would be left for me to work as vicar alongside the Rector, the Revd. Glynne Turner. I accepted the invitation to move to this new benefice because it meant extra responsibilities for me but I confess that I did have private reservations as to the workability of what was proposed. My special role would be to minister to the Welsh-speaking congregation in the parish church of Ystradyfodwg (St. John Baptist) there being a faithful but mainly elderly group of about twenty worshippers. In the 1970's there was still a good sprinkling of Welsh to be heard among the older generation in Rhondda and several Welsh chapels were still very much a force to be reckoned with in the community.

To put the whole situation in perspective, some years after the benefice was created the whole picture was transformed because it was decided that St. John's had to be demolished due to problems of subsidence, and St. David's Ton Pentre had to be dismantled due to its crumbling bath stone structure. Instead a modern church was erected on the site of the old St. John's church to serve the community of Ton Pentre and the mission church of St. Mark's at Gelli was closed. The parish of Ystradyfodwg today is served by one incumbent with responsibility for the two churches, one in Pentre and the other in Ton Pentre. In other words, the parish priest who is there today has the same parish responsibilities that I had as "team vicar" in the 1970's. The benefice "set-up" died a death finally in the early 1990's. With the benefit of hindsight one could say that a more thorough investigation of the structural condition and feasibility of retaining the four church buildings would have resulted in the idea of the need for a Rectorial Benefice questionable. As it was, the Benefice continued through the 1970's and 1980's with an unsettling coming and going of clergy, clearly frustrated by their status and the apparent confusion among ordinary parishioners in general about the alleged benefits of the benefice. The result of this lack of continuity of clergy and the reduction of buildings led inevitably to the decision to "wind up" what had been in my opinion a misguided initiative from the start. I truly believe that the dye was cast when at the outset the "third" parish withdrew from the set-up leaving just the two "units" to work together. It takes at least three to make up a satisfactory "team" situation in reality.

Despite these disparaging thoughts there were a number of valuable aspects to the Rectorial Benefice situation. Glynne and I were in our "home" churches every Sunday morning but once a month we took Evensong in the "away" churches, which was an opportunity for both clergy and congregations to enjoy a change of scene and a change of voice! It was also good to be able to share problems of a pastoral nature and, for me especially, as someone developing his ministry, to learn from someone of Glynne's experience about parish administration etc. The first year into the benefice I was given the challenge of taking the Good Friday

Three hours Devotional Service. This was my first big "hurdle" with regard to conducting an important service, my previous experience of this service being on the "receiving end" only! It is a gruelling service to have to take as regards duration but it can be refreshing spiritually for the person leading it. In fact after the first hour is completed, the time moves along quite quickly (maybe not for the congregation!) and then, lo and behold, the final meditation has arrived and you feel that you are in a state of panic to finish before the three hours are up! It was good to be able to share the Confirmation preparation classes for the young people too. We as clergy took various aspects of the course in turns; while the one led the class, the other listened in and joined in the discussion when appropriate. Mind you, all these positive things can be very much part of a "Team Ministry" arrangement, which for me is a far more constructive approach than binding congregations together simply for the sake of justifying the existence of a united benefice. As clergy we can surely share good practice and pool talents without the hassle and disorder of a united benefice. The apostle Paul speaks very movingly about sharing our talents as Christians when he says, *"There are different kinds of gifts but the same Spirit,"* but creating unnecessary administrative complications and the blurring of identities surely undermines this principle.

We were fortunate in having an almost newly built house at Maindy Grove in Ton Pentre and, unlike the situation in Pontypridd, it was right in the centre of the community rather than at the top of a steep hill above the town. The only problem was that the back garden had a very steep gradient. No chance of growing vegetables or roses here, only a few colourful bushes to brighten up the scene. One day we noticed a few deep holes in the ground at the top end of the garden, then, on another occasion, we espied a light brown creature emerging from one of the holes. We had a nest of weasels as neighbours! We also often had the company of the renowned Rhondda sheep down from the hills rummaging into our refuse bins and, when the mood took them, upturning them to allow a more thorough scrutiny. Talk about the T.V. series, "All creatures great and small!" It was enough to make James Herriott jealous! However the "sheep" that were under my care were much more responsive to human contact, the community being friendliness itself. A good deal has been recorded about the warm, close-knit mining communities of South Wales. True, by the 1970's, there were changes to the industrial and social scene to cause a threat to the pattern of "togetherness", but there was still a hearty and genuine "Welcome in the hillsides" to be felt and seen in the Rhondda.

Fortunately, Sheila's school was now only a short step away in the next valley and she continued to enjoy her time there. Her work with church music went on apace, building on a sound choral tradition in St. Peter's, Pentre. At least we did not have to initiate a choir here, just develop the interest that was already present in a core of faithful choristers. We needed to attract some more children's voices and to increase the numbers in our Sunday school. It was remarkably easy to gain the support of parents of young people. I even managed to secure the support of some young altar servers. Of course, unlike at Glyncoch, there was already a solid generation of churchgoers to form a sound base for expansion. The problem arose, "Can we introduce new ideas without upsetting the established, faithful band? In that sense, a missionary situation like Glyncoch, being a kind of "virgin soil" was easier for a gardener to cultivate, because there was little danger of "overturning a largely empty wheelbarrow", as it were.

St. Peter's, as a building, was a case of Victoriana at its best or worst, depending on your viewpoint. It was often referred to as the "Cathedral of the Rhondda". Its elaborate flight of stone steps guiding you through the iron portals of its porch, together with its extensive grounds, laid to lawn, brought echoes of an age that appreciated a spot of elegance and grandeur among the coal pit-heads and rows of terraced houses. Here one could glimpse for a while the God of majesty and awe whose Holy Temple had to be as high and spacious as possible to encourage its inhabitants to sing with more gusto than ever the words of the hymn *"Nearer my God to Thee, nearer to Thee!"* It was indeed a fine edifice of its kind, but terribly difficult to heat and very expensive to maintain, of course. The great figure who strode its stage for most of the first half of the twentieth century was Canon William Lewis. By his evangelical fervour and charismatic personality he had dominated the spiritual life of Pentre and much of the Rhondda Fawr for many years. Some of that eloquent proclaiming of the Gospel was still to be detected in the hearty, dignified worship that was part of the legacy Canon Lewis handed down to the generations that followed. Every festival traditionally had its Anthem sung by the choir. Evensong was still a fully sung service and almost as well attended as the morning Eucharist.

When I first arrived at St. Peter's, the west window, which was about eighty feet high, had been the victim of storm damage and was in a very sorry state. Faced by this problem I managed to enlist the help of Tim Lewis, the Principal of Swansea College of Art. He initiated a college student project to replace the broken panes of stained glass in their correct sequence (fortunately we had a very good set of photographs of all the church windows to refer to). Within six months the impressive west window was back to its former glory. I was so glad that Tim happened to be an enthusiastic admirer of Victorian stained glass and proved it by his expertise on our behalf.

We found that the good people of the parish were extremely fond of trips to places of interest. We would organise excursions to St. Fagan's Museum of Welsh Life (as it is now called) near Cardiff, pantomimes and fruit picking afternoons in the vicinity of Hereford. All good fun and excellent for building up social contact and opening the door to non-churchgoers to join us for fellowship.

One rather exceptional Saturday I well remember. It was the only time in my ministry when I had to take a funeral immediately followed by a wedding! The funeral was that of a former church warden of St. Peters, Fred Lisle, for whose service the church was almost full, such was the respect in which Fred was held. Within an hour of the funeral congregation having dispersed in their sober dress the wedding guests were arriving in their finery. It was a most odd experience changing one's disposition from one of sympathy and solemnity for the one role and joy and brightness for the other. By the time the wedding was over I felt like taking off my two masks! How fortunate that I did not confuse Fred's favourite hymn which we sang at his funeral,

"Fight the good fight with all thy might", with any of the hymns at the wedding!

One family home whose acquaintance I made on my first round of visits to the parish was that of the Scott sisters; the three were living together in Maindy Crescent. One was widowed and the other two were spinsters. I was advised to make prior arrangements to call on them rather than visit "on spec", as it were. I should have realised from the rather formal invitation that I received to "take tea with them at 4 o'clock prompt, please" what was in store for me. It was really like a scene from the 1940's. There was the tiered cake stand with daintily cut cucumber sandwiches, queen cakes and slices of jam sponge (all home-made, of course) and tea served immaculately from fine china cups. Conversation was conducted in a genteel, very refined fashion. *"I hope you will settle comfortably here, Vicar, we are all very friendly, you know, when you get to know us. Oh! Please do have another cucumber sandwich. I made them especially, as we do not have the pleasure of a vicar to tea very often!"* I had never before experienced such an unconventional ambience in a home. I was in the Rhondda valley, famous for its coal mines, colliery waste tips and very "down-to-earth" mentality, but it felt more like the "Barchester Towers" of Anthony Trollope fame. I was confident that this experience would be a "one-off" event and would never come my way again. I have to admit though that those cucumber sandwiches were delicious!

We held two splendid Church Summer Fairs in the grounds of St. Peter's during our time in the Rhondda. They bore testimony to the excellent way in which church members worked well together for a common aim. It was a lovely spectacle seeing such imposing church grounds decked with stalls and dotted with people seated at tables enjoying refreshments while chatting happily. These occasions involved a lot of work, admittedly, but there is much to be said for holding an event in which men, women and children can all join to make a contribution to its success. The other point about these fund-raising events is that they are an opportunity for the whole community to help towards the church's financial maintenance while also putting church activity "on the map" in the locality. Fortunately the vicar's plea to the Almighty to grant us fair weather was granted on both occasions.

It was during my time in the Rhondda that I was invited to join the group of Diocesan Inspectors of church schools. One of the original members of our team of six clergy was the then vicar of Cwmafan, the Revd. Huw Jones, who was later to become Dean of Brecon and finally Bishop of St. Davids. Our remit as inspectors was to conduct an annual inspection of the Voluntary Aided and Voluntary Controlled schools owned by the diocese in order to monitor standards in the teaching and learning of Religious Education and the quality of the presentation of Collective worship (School Assembly) and also to evaluate the spiritual, moral, social and cultural development of pupils. This was quite a demanding task but, as a qualified teacher, an interesting and valued one for me. The worst aspect was the writing up of reports of our findings afterwards. Fortunately, another of the inspectors was the vicar of Cwmparc (the next parish to Ton Pentre), the Revd. Lawrence Miles, a dear, kindly man with whom I shared journeys to schools in which we were both involved and to the meetings of the panel of inspectors. I valued Lawrence's friendship in serving the schools together in this way. This contact with church schools was to play a greater part in my ministry later on in my career and I valued keeping up to date with the church school scene.

It was with some sadness that after just three years I felt the inevitable need now to be responsible for my own parish. The realisation that we were to leave the Rhondda in which we had felt so much at home was a painful one. I had seen an advertisement in the "Church Times" for an incumbent in the Diocese of Swansea and Brecon for which Welsh was essential. Of course, were I to succeed in being appointed, Sheila would need to apply for a teaching post near to where we were to move. Movement towards these two possible ends was now set in motion. The appointment to Llandeilo Talybont (Pontarddulais) was the nomination of the Provincial Board, which meant that clergy from outside the diocese of the vacant parish, if thought suitable, would be given priority. Thus I had a good chance of being considered. My first task however was to discuss these thoughts with my bishop. The interview with Bishop Eryl was the most uncomfortable that I have ever endured with any bishop. I was accused of betraying the diocese, of seeking a parish that was most "unsuited to me" and of having a "cavalier" attitude towards my present commitments. Despite my claim that Pontarddulais would offer me the opportunity to minister in a fully bilingual community and describing my frustration with aspects of the situation in which I was working, the atmosphere between us was somewhat heated. I pointed out that I had been far happier working as a curate with clear responsibilities under a vicar than being a vicar with questionable responsibilities alongside a rector. It was after my appointment to Llandeilo Talybont was announced that a rather peevish paragraph appeared in the "Welsh Churchman" calling on the Provincial Board of Patronage not to "make their prey" on the Welsh-speaking clergy of the Llandaff diocese. Today thankfully there is a less "insular" approach to clergy moving around and, with a greater dearth of clergy these days (especially those proficient in Welsh) "beggars can't be choosers!" Bishops today are more sensitive to the individual needs and talents of their clergy and wish to address them by deploying them more effectively. In the Church's continuing mission to serve the people of Wales we have all learned to see things in sharper perspective. Of course, in my case, it was three weeks after the tense interview with Bishop Eryl in July 1975 that his sad resignation from the see of Llandaff was announced. I truly believe that, in retrospect, he was under a considerable emotional strain when we spoke together and this had an impact on his handling of the interview. His departure was a tragic end to a faithful ministry spent in three of the dioceses of the Province, commanding the respect of all who knew him and worked with him.

Meanwhile Sheila and I made our way to Ely Tower in Brecon, the home of the bishop of Swansea and Brecon, where both of us had a warm welcome from Bishop and Mrs John Thomas. I had met Bishop John's son, David, when I took the Welsh classes in St. Michael's College where he had arrived as a member of staff. After my "cosy chat" with Bishop John and

Sheila's heart to heart chat with Mrs Thomas, we could settle our minds to a move west. We were still on tenterhooks that Sheila's application to a teaching post in Gorseinon would be successful. Within three weeks our prayers were answered. She had secured a post in Penyrheol Comprehensive, a large school of some 1,400 pupils. Its head teacher was in fact an Anglican, being a Reader from the parish of St. David's, Neath. So we had both secured new positions in West Glamorgan. We were exchanging an area where "steam coal" was king for the place where "anthracite" ruled the way!

I recall a lady who had been a devout secretary of her Independent chapel in Ton Pentre, on hearing that we had decided to leave the area, telephoning to urge me to think again and saying how rare it was to have someone my age ministering in Welsh in the Rhondda. She waxed lyrically about the importance of the survival of the language within the Church and the culture of the Rhondda and how vital it was that we retain the few Welsh-speaking clergy that we had. It was kind of her to be so concerned about the mission of the Church and broad-minded of her to see the Church situation as a whole and not from a purely denominational point of view. Nevertheless I did my best to explain that using the Welsh language more extensively was one of the reasons why I felt I had to spread my wings further afield. It was with heavy hearts that we left the Rhondda valley and its lovely people who were so ready to "pull together" and support all you tried to do. The valley boy and his lady were moving west but were not to turn their backs entirely on their home diocese for a while yet.

CHAPTER 6

MY FIRST INCUMBENCY

We may have left the Diocese of Llandaff under somewhat of a cloud but the summer of 1975 greeted us with blue skies and high temperatures. Fair play to the good people of the Rhondda, our men for all seasons, Roy Brabham and Ray Davies, who had always been ready to give a helping hand about the church or at the vicarage, helped us move our belongings to what was a typically large vicarage of the mid-Victorian era.

St. Teilo's church, Pontarddulais

Not from the Rhondda was there any hint of small-mindedness at our leaving them for pastures new. They were reliable to the last and we as clergy are always grateful to those, like Roy and Ray, who roll up their sleeves and act the Christian part when it is most needed.

The vicarage, like the church adjacent to it, dated from 1853. It was set in its own immense grounds, complete with double drive and lawns to the front and the one side of the house together with a large enclosed garden at the rear. For the gardener there was too much of a good thing! One immediate job faced us before actually moving in. It would be to our benefit to buy a good stock of coal at summer prices ready for the winter to feed the coal-fired Rayburn in the main living room (which we were always to call the Rayburn room). So it was on one hot, August day that I shifted three tons of the best Tumble coal and afterwards enjoyed the delights of a long soak in the bath of a neighbour's house, the home of Dan and Addie Thomas, since we had not yet taken up residence in the parish. What a novel way to get to know your first parishioners. Have a bath in their house! – having been given their permission first, of course.

The vicarage had two staircases – one main staircase leading from the front door spiralling upstairs in elegant mode, the other was the original servants' stairs inside the back door, leading to two bedrooms on a slightly lower level (naturally!) than the main upstairs bedrooms. It reminded me very much of the T.V. series "Upstairs and Downstairs". This was especially so of the set of electric bells attached to the wall of the Rayburn room intended to summon the servants to some household duty at the behest of the vicar or vicar's wife. Strange to say, whenever we tried using the push-bell in our bedroom, we never had a response from any servant below!

The front hall was so massive that we held a number of sales of work, coffee mornings etc. towards the cost of the Church Hall, whose plans had been earmarked and prepared on the drawing-board but not yet acted upon. These were the only occasions in my whole ministry when we were grateful for a large house! It was certainly a house of character in which it was not difficult to imagine the Victorian parson gathered round the roaring fire in the huge lounge on a winter's evening while the housekeeper and her maid cleared away the supper things and prepared the breakfast table before retiring to bed. Those were the days! Yet now there were to be no servants, there was no gardener in sight, only less time to make up for their absence. Moreover the heating bills could not be avoided! Such was the lot of those who in the late twentieth century had to cope with huge vicarages built in and geared for a completely different era and lifestyle. These large parsonages are gradually being replaced, thankfully.

The community of Pontarddulais grew as a result of the coming to the area of coal, tin and bricks (the remains of an old brick-works was still to be seen close behind the vicarage garden).The old railway track taking coal from the colliery up in the hills above the town still straddles the main Swansea road out of the town near Babell chapel. Yet the industrial invasion clearly trespassed on to peaceful, rural surroundings. The farms and smallholdings were not far away. In the 1970's Welsh and English rivalled one another as the first language of its inhabitants. Today, perhaps with the increase of new housing developments and the eclipse of the old industries, English is beginning to gain the upper hand. In some ways the town has gradually become a distant dormitory residential township for the city of Swansea. When we took up residence the busy A48 road passed through the town. You crossed it at your peril except at rush-hour times and on Saturdays in the summer when you could saunter across between vehicles gridlocked on route to the resorts of West Wales. About six months after we moved in the last stretch of the M4 as far as Pont Abraham was built and Pontarddulais at last escaped the endless flow of through traffic.

The parish had two churches – well three, to be exact, because the ancient parish church of Llandeilo Taybont (known locally as "The church on the marsh") was by then in disuse, leaving the church of St.Teilo, adjoining the vicarage, providing services in Welsh and the church of St. Michael and All Angels, built in 1892, to provide services for the large intake of English-speaking inhabitants who had found work in the local community from far and wide. Until several years before my arrival there had been another church in use, St. Martin's at Grovesend, on the way to Gorseinon, but this building had been sold. Just before my appointment to the parish was made, the diocese annexed St. Anne's church in Pontlliw, which had also been part of the parish, to the neighbouring parish of Penllergaer.

I well remember the vicar's warden at St. Michael's, Tommy Davies, drawing me aside soon after our arrival in the parish and saying, *"Do you want a piece of advice, Vicar?"* *"Of course, Tommy,"* I replied, *"as a newcomer, any advice would be much appreciated."*

"Well", he said, *"the congregation in St. Michael's is made up almost entirely of two families, the Evans's and the Downings. If you upset one of either family, the whole lot will take umbrage. So if I were you, I would bite your tongue before using it, unless you know exactly who you are talking to!"* Actually people were not as "prickly" as he made out, but it was sound advice to adhere to in any close-knit community. Tommy and his wife, Kate, were great characters. He looked after his garden, vegetables included, until he was well into his nineties. When I was in their house one day Tommy got up from his chair at about 3 p.m. and announced, *"Well, I must be off now, my friends at the Hollies* (home for the elderly) *will be expecting me for a chat to cheer them up a bit."* Tommy was then ninety one himself! Kate had a good, strong alto voice and was a faithful member of St. Michael's choir. Naturally Sheila was happy to take responsibility for the church choir. She always said that this choir had the best range of voices of all the parishes in which we served, before and after. We had 3 tenors, 3 basses, 4 altos, a good number of sopranos and several children's voices. Most of the adults were already in the choir when we arrived. St. Teilo's also had a strong female choir led by the organist, Elwyn Jones, who was a keen musician. The Sunday school was about eighty strong with about ten in the adult class. The Mothers' Union numbered sixty on the books and we had a small Men's Working Party ready to do a blitz on any practical job needed around the churches and in the churchyard at St. Teilo's.

Just before the Church Hall was erected we held a meeting of the Ladies Guild who had succeeded in doing so much to raise funds for the Building Project.

At this meeting I had my first ever "contretemps" with a parish group. It was a situation that I am sure many of us who are married clergy have faced in our career. Discussing who should take a lead in various parish activities, one of the group, no doubt voicing the opinions of many, declared, *"You see, Vicar, the vicar's wife has always seen to the altar linen and been in charge of the altar flower list and has automatically assumed the role of Enrolling Member of the Mothers' Union branch."* I realized that some straight talking was needed here, so I replied, *"The vicar's wife happens to be my wife and my wife, like everyone else, has her own talents and interests. Has the vicar's wife in this parish ever taken the church choir? Has she taken an interest in flower arranging?"* The silence that followed was deafening! Then I added, *"I trust my wife to do what she feels capable of doing and what she wants to do. I would not dream of asking any of you good ladies to take on any task that you feel you cannot do. After all, it is all voluntary work."* End of story.

The problem lay basically in the fact that the parish had never before had the experience of a vicar with a wife who had a working career and, in that sense, a life of her own to lead. Parishioners had to adapt to a changing situation, as all of us have to in so many circumstances in life. What I was determined to establish from the outset was that we must not mentally place people into "fixed slots" of our own surmising. Once this point was accepted and understood, all tension in the meeting was released and harmony reigned from then on. The result of all this was that several tasks traditionally associated with "the vicar's wife" were duly delegated! It is strange but true that in no other profession is there any supposition of the role of the spouse of the professional, for example, "the doctor's wife" pigeon holed for this or that job. Yet a pedestal was assumed to be where a clergyman's wife belonged!

One major task that clergy have to address is the encouragement of our people to fulfil the gifts that God has given them to be used in his service. Thankfully the days are gone (or almost gone!) when the vicar (and possibly his wife also) delighted in the status of "running the show" and treating parishioners as "pew fodder" who are perpetually at the receiving end of his ministrations. Now the traffic is refreshingly "two-way" with the parish priest aiming at *enabling* the people to be what they are called to be *"a chosen people, a royal priesthood."* This new emphasis on the ministry of all God's people should not be prompted by the current situation of decreasing clerical manpower but by the whole nature and purpose of the Church and its mission.

When the Church Hall was completed, it was officially opened by the widow of a former incumbent of the parish, Mrs Wilma Hilary-Jones and dedicated by the Archdeacon of Gower, the Venerable Harry Williams. After leaving Pontarddulais Canon Hilary-Jones became the Rector of St. Andrew's Major, near Dinas Powys. Once up and running, our church hall was used quite extensively. One of the new ideas that Sheila and I launched was the setting up of a Parish Fellowship group. All too often a parish functions on a social level in single-gender units; seldom do both sexes meet on a regular basis. We invited speakers of general interest and activities were arranged that brought husbands and wives together, including trips to places of interest, stage productions etc. It was from this mixed Fellowship group that the idea of the Fellowship Singers was born, under Sheila's direction. This was basically a Glee Party that sang popular songs of the 30's and 40's, drawn entirely from our Fellowship group – strictly no guest artists! The purpose of this venture was two-fold; (a) to promote fellowship while practising the songs. Often we sang songs of a humorous kind. I remember participating in one song as a member of three couples in which the lady sat on the gentleman's knee while he sang to her *"If you were the only girl in the world,"* remembering that I was about thirty six at the time and the partner on my knee to whom I was singing was at least seventy! During one of our concerts an irrepressible titter was caused by one of the Glee Party doing a special rendering of the familiar ditty, "Champagne Charlie is my name." This "Charlie" insisted on confusing the two different sounds for the letters "ch", so we had the word, "Champagne" pronounced as the "ch" in the word "cheese" and the word "Charlie" pronounced as the "sh" in the word "shop!" It was a unique version indeed, to everyone's amusement. Bless his cotton socks!

However the greater aim of setting up this singing group was (b) to take the Church into the community by entertaining at homes for the elderly, Senior Citizens Groups, Harvest Suppers etc. Thus it was an enjoyable "letting down of hair" while being a useful exercise in outreach into the community. On reflection, I suppose it was quite an exceptional example of outreach really.

When the Church Hall became available to us the Sunday Schools in both churches combined to form one gathering in the Hall on Sunday afternoon. Once a month we had a Family Service which took the form of a simplified Morning Prayer in which the children were encouraged to participate. It was both surprising and pleasing to have the full support of all the regular worshippers at this service. It is often the case that some "regulars" simply boycott a Family Service claiming that it is "for *them* and not for *us*." At one service in St. Michael's I recall an example of how attentive one "regular" was to what was being said from the pulpit. To begin my talk I asked the congregation to put their hands up if they had a birthday that week. One elderly lady joined two of the children in obediently putting her hand up. On being asked how old she would be on her birthday she replied, "*84 years young, Vicar!*" (*"Whoever does not receive the Kingdom of God like a child will never enter it."* were the words of Jesus that came to my mind, immediately.) I invited everyone in church to join in singing "Happy Birthday".to the brave lady who put her hand up. There is a place for informality in worship, especially when, as in these Family services, we are anxious to attract a firmer commitment from those not claiming to be "churched". The Sunday school was a strong feature of parish life throughout my ministry in Pontarddulais. Much of this was due to the close family ties and the more responsible role taken by caring parents that you find in the more Welsh-speaking parts of South Wales, in my experience.

An enjoyable and much cherished custom was started originally because of the need of funds for the church hall building project, namely, a group of carollers from our churches giving up their time over the weeks before Christmas to tour the area singing. By singing I mean

singing *all* the verses of *"O come, all ye faithful"* etc.
We had our hymn sheets in front of us with descanters
ready to blend with those singing melody for some of
the verses. I think it was because we sang with a little
more care and polish than many who went out carolling
that most people looked forward to our visit as a kind
of "treat." Our last port of call on the very last night of
singing was at the very top of the parish where the road
began to approach Garnswllt – the home of Mr and
Mrs David Last. Mr Last was the manager of the former
Multiflex Company, then sited in Llanelli. We were
always treated to mince pies and mulled wine (or soft
drinks for the children) by our hosts, that is, *after* we
had sung our carols! Mrs Last Senior, aged over eighty,
a regular worshipper at church, stayed up especially to
hear us and joined in the singing like a child who had
just been given the thrill of her life in return for being so
well-behaved! What a shame that the simple joys of
socialising in festive mood have gradually disappeared
today, pushed aside by the self-contained mentality
created by the age of television comforts. I really felt the
true spirit of Christmas to be at work in the human
contact and fun produced by our carolling sessions. It
was worth the effort braving the cold and rain! – even
though one year I caught a dose of 'flu!

Having been in the parish about six months, I was
introduced to a Licensed Reader, Leonard Fry, (a native
of Penclawdd on Gower), whose working career had
taken him to Cheshire to live. However, since retiring to
the Pontarddulais area, Len had never functioned as a
Reader. I invited him to apply for a renewal of his
licence. Thereafter he was a great help to me and an
asset to the parish. I learned that in fact Len had sought

ordination in his younger days but was refused by the Diocese of Chester on the assumption that, academically, he would not be able to cope with New Testament Greek and the rigours of the philosophical aspects of Christian Doctrine. Sometimes I wonder whether we, as a Church, do not put unnecessary obstacles in the way of some potentially sound applicants for ordination. Here was a man capable of taking a service with clarity and dignity, of expounding from the pulpit with confidence and conviction, while possessing a warm, approachable personality, not to mention a dry, homely wit as a bonus. Such a person would have been an ideal candidate for a pattern of local ministry which is gradually emerging now within the life of the Church. An example of Len's wit was illustrated one Sunday morning when we had the company of Robert, one of the residents of the Hollies, who invariably came into church during the first hymn, simply because of the meals situation at the residential home, and sat in the very first row of the nave! This particular morning, having come down from the pulpit (we still used the pulpit to preach from, unlike many churches today who, for some reason, regard it with distaste), as I passed Robert to make my way back to my stall, he pushed something into my hand. When I got to my stall I glanced at the object given to me. It was none other than a "Taxi" bar of chocolate. Looking over my shoulder from his place in the chancel, Len chortled, *"I bet that's the first time you've taken a taxi from the pulpit to your stall, vicar!"*

During our time in the parish our music repertoire was supplemented by the choirs of both churches being affiliated to the Royal School of Church Music. Through this link we had the opportunity to join other church choirs for singing practices towards the annual Choral Festival held in Brecon Cathedral in May and an Advent Carol Service in the Swansea area, all under the enthusiastic and competent baton of David Gedge, organist and choirmaster at Brecon. These were not just enjoyable musical occasions but also opportunities for sharing with other parishes and thus providing us with an insight into the whole Diocesan scene. Parish life can be claustrophobic. It is like a breath of fresh air to make contact with groups from other parishes and share experiences.

Referring to diocesan events prompts me to recall a Diocesan Mothers' Union Festival at Brecon when I was asked by the then Dean, the Very Revd. Ungoed Jacob, to assist with the laying up of the M.U. banners at the start of the service. As I laid up one banner on my side of the sanctuary, I was appalled to see the banner which a colleague had apparently safely placed against the wall, beginning to totter. In a matter of seconds there was an almighty crash, as banner collapsed against banner and fell down like a pack of cards. The resulting chaos was as nothing compared with the consternation on the faces of the banner bearers during the Recessional Hymn at the end of the service when each one received every banner but that of her own branch. There must have been quite an "unholy" mess to sort out afterwards for each banner to reach its rightful destination. Even in cathedral worship things do not always work like clockwork!

One of the tasks that Bishop Benjamin Vaughan asked me to undertake over and above my parish work was to act as Secretary of the Welsh section of

Covenanting Churches in the Swansea area. In the aftermath of the decision in 1976 to set up a Covenant in Wales between the Church in Wales, the Wesleyan Methodist Church, the United Reformed Church, The Presbyterian church and some Baptist churches, a pledge was made that these churches grow together in understanding, fellowship and worship. With regard to worship, a Covenanting Rite of Holy Communion was compiled for use at ecumenical gatherings. The Diocese of Swansea and Brecon, in company with other dioceses, set up a working party for English and Welsh-speaking areas. The Welsh-speaking areas in our Diocese were located mainly in the Cwmtawe (Swansea valley) and Llwchwr (covering the Loughor estuary area) deaneries.

One of the advantages of our deanery of Llwchwr was that we were only six parishes. Being a small deanery, we were encouraged to work together as a team towards deanery projects, share prayer time together, establish a strong Sunday School Teachers' Association and a Men's Society. We were small enough to identify easily with one another, yet large enough to make it viable to meet in such numbers that we could share problems and thus widen the boundaries limited to a parish in a positive way. I should think that in today's Church situation the Llwchwr deanery would fit well into the envisaged pattern for a viable Ministry Area in which a "team spirit" among clergy was a realistic goal that could be achieved. I was privileged to act as Rural Dean of Llwchwr from 1979 to 1983. One of my deanery colleagues was the then vicar of Gorseinon, The Revd. Saunders Davies, who succeeded me as Rural Dean before moving to the Diocese of

Bangor to be eventually elected Bishop of Bangor. Another colleague was the Revd. Howard Jones, now assisting in the parish of Llanelli. We were a very happy, collaborative deanery and I know that the same is true of the Llwchwr Deanery today. It was my privilege on one occasion to introduce the then Dean of Brecon to our diocesan conference and congratulate him on his appointment that week as the new Bishop of St. Asaph (and later Archbishop of Wales) He was of course Archbishop Alwyn Rice-Jones.

One of the duties that fell to the Rural Dean (who is today given the title of "Area Dean") was to meet with the Bishop and fellow Rural Deans each month to discuss issues of importance to the diocese. At the first of these meetings I made the acquaintance of the Rector of Penmaen, who was the Rural Dean of Gower. His name was Canon Iorrie Richards. Everyone called him Iorrie but his proper name was a bit of a tongue-twister, Iorwerth. He was greatly loved not only in his parish but throughout the Gower, where he had spent most of his ministry. He did not drive a car but delighted to walk as often as circumstances allowed around his parish as the true pastor of his flock. Usually I took him to the meetings in Brecon which gave us an opportunity to get well acquainted. When he retired he and Dilys returned to his native Llanelli. He had been brought up in St. Alban's Church in the town. Just a year before his return to Llanelli I had arrived in the area as vicar of Felinfoel (see Chapter 8). When Iorrie was not helping out at churches in the area (Dilys would drive him everywhere), they would come and worship at Felinfoel where they made many friends. After some years Dilys died very suddenly, Iorrie surviving her by several years.

They were buried in Felinfoel churchyard. Iorrie was a parish priest of the "old style", completely unassuming and gentle in manner, a man who served his people joyfully – a great example to his fellow clergy.

One tradition in the parish that I had inherited which I was anxious to do something about was the fact that the two churches never met together except for Harvest Thanksgiving and Carol Services. I resolved to start a monthly bilingual service in each church alternately. Amazingly, there were a handful of people in both churches who during a whole lifetime had never crossed the threshold of the "other" church except for a rare funeral service. The reason was not just one of loyalty to a building but also to a language. But was it loyalty to Christ and his Family, the Church? I think not. Although some stubbornly stayed away from the monthly service when it was held in the "away" church (as so often happens), the majority of the congregations found this widening of fellowship in worship refreshing. One cannot please everyone all the time! You cannot even try!

Another move to extend the parish "parameters" was to share Bible study courses during the period of Lent with our Wesleyan Methodist friends. We began holding an occasional united service together through the co-operation of the Revd. Emrys Evans, minister of Triniti. This was to develop on the lines of the Act of Covenant between Churches in Wales mentioned already. I recall that at the first of these services held in St. Teilo's church, one of the members of St.Teilo's, astonished to see a long established Wesleyan friend of hers coming into her church, could not help but remark, *"What on earth are you doing here?"* To which her

Wesleyan friend chirpily answered, *"The same as you, worshipping God!"* Some eyebrows were raised at first at this "coming together" because Pontarddulais was for many years a bastion of Nonconformity. In fact there were no less than four ministers in post residing in the town during my time there. However, this move to bring two denominations closer together, added to an established ecumenical fraternal of ministers and a combined all-church effort towards Christian Aid Week, apart from generally supporting the "big occasions" in individual churches, made for a strong sense of Christian fellowship in the community. This spirit of mutual support continues today, which includes our Roman Catholic friends. Some years after I left the parish they had to abandon their church building because of a serious building defect, using St. Michael's church until their new building was completed. What are Christian friends for?

One of the tasks in which I was invited to be involved by Bishop Vaughan was to be a member of the Swansea Religious Broadcasting Committee for the local Radio Station programmes. This involved co-ordinating epilogue talks in Welsh and arranging venues for broadcast services to be held in Welsh for the area covered by the station. One of the unexpected "perks" was to attend a Religious Broadcasting Training Course in Bushey outside London. I was able to arrange accommodation with my former Theological College chaplain, Michael Bowles, who was by now vicar of Stanmore. The reunion with him and his wife proved as beneficial, if not more beneficial, to me as the course itself! Still the whole insight into the field of broadcasting was a reminder of the challenge it poses to the Church with regard to communicating its message through the media as effectively as possible today. It was a salient reminder to me, even in the 1970's, of the age of "mass media" we had reached and how the Church had to respond to it effectively.

Christmas 1978 was rather a "non-event" for us for a family reason. Gran had sustained two strokes early in December. I had been to see her at home on Christmas Eve. She was weak but lucid in mind. Sheila and I decided that after morning services and a quick lunch on Christmas Day we would go to Pontypridd and see how things were. As we were sitting down to eat our midday meal the telephone rang. I knew it was the news we were dreading. Gran had passed away at 11.30 a.m. on Christmas morning, aged eighty six. She had suffered from phlebitis in the leg for some years but, on the whole, had got around very well for her advancing age. She was eighty four before finally giving up her Sunday school duties. I will always remember when we first took her and my mother-in-law to see the vicarage at Pontarddulais just before we actually moved in. The grass was about four feet high around the side of the house. Gran and Mabel were sitting against the wall and we could only see their hats turning to each other as they chatted in the jungle that surrounded them. Yes – on Christmas Day 1978 a great light which had guided my life was extinguished, but some lovely memories live on, thank God.

Sadly, in 1979 a terrible tragedy beset our neighbouring village of Hendy, when the church was destroyed as a result of arson. While a new building was being planned, the congregation at St. David's church, Hendy, crossed the Dulais Bridge to share our building at St. Michael's. This meant that a diocesan gulf was being bridged since Hendy was then part of the parish of Llanedi and Tycroes within the Diocese of St. Davids. The diocesan boundary was of course the River Loughor. Many diocesan boundaries divide communities which socially and at local authority levels form identifiable units. Nevertheless, when a crisis like the one that unfortunately overtook Hendy church was concerned, it is the Christian community, not the diocesan divide, that takes priority, witnessing to Christian mission.

I have already mentioned that the ancient parish church of Llandeilo Talybont was in a state of disuse. It had held its last service some five years before my arrival in the parish. The church was in too remote a location for there to be any further use for it, apart from the funds needed to put in place its structural needs, renew almost all the furnishings and, not least, continue to maintain the building adequately in the future. Its parlous and vulnerable condition and the dilemma of what to do about its future was an item for discussion at many meetings of the Parochial Church Council while I was incumbent. The first time I visited the church was, believe it or not, on Christmas Day 1975. As it was one of those clear, crisp winter days and had been fairly dry for some weeks, Sheila and I decided after our traditional Christmas lunch to make our way through the muddy fields to the banks of the River Loughor to the dilapidated churchyard and entered the church porch. I had heard about its dreadful state due to a combination of weather infiltration, theft of lead from the roof and sheer vandalism during the last few years. However, seeing the chaos for ourselves was something else. The roof was leaking badly everywhere, cattle had entered and caused complete disarray and items of furniture, Bibles and service books had been wantonly destroyed by vandals. The church was at the mercy of the elements and human callousness and, the building being so far from human contact in the community at large, we were powerless to prevent its inevitable disintegration.

We were left utterly depressed by what we saw. However today that same building stands as an example of a late medieval church in all its pre-Reformation glory in St. Fagan's Museum of Welsh Life, Cardiff. This transformation is a testimony to the Resurrection message if ever there was. The fascinating story of its evolvement from calamity to national heritage deserves special treatment which is included in Chapter 10.

One character stands out in my memories of the many I was privileged to know and serve in Pontarddulais. This was the tall, gaunt, white-haired member of St. Teilo's and familiar, much respected member of the community, John S. Davies. "John S." as he was familiarly known, had been the manager of the Coated Metals Works in the town, a big employer in its day. Nowadays a substantial new housing complex has been erected on the site of the old works. "John S." was a man of considerable learning. It was a trial of strength gaining access to the living room of his house in Tynybonau Road, so jammed full was the hallway with magazines, periodicals and books dating back decades. I pitied his poor wife in her attempts at keeping the dust at bay! He may have been somewhat eccentric in his demeanour and ways but he was a true gentleman in the proper sense of the word, - a gentle man of quiet but impressive integrity. He attended the funerals of as many former employees and acquaintances as he could, often being seen walking the ten miles to Swansea Crematorium to pay his last respects to departed friends. He seemed to belong to another age, an age in which people had time to give to their fellow human beings without a trace of the patronising air of the "do-gooder". If he was an example of the industrial manager of yesteryear for whom relationships in industry involved personal concern and respect for employer and employee, we are today much the poorer for their slow eclipse.

1981 was a momentous year for the Church in Wales. That year celebrated the 60 years of its Disestablishment from the Church of England. A special open-air service was held in what was then Cardiff Arms Park (now the Millennium Stadium) to mark this momentous occasion. Unfortunately, "yours truly" missed the boat, not through lack of interest, but because of an unfortunate accident to my foot! A few weeks before the event I was mowing the front lawn and along its one length was a short grassy bank. After about half an hour's mowing I must have lost concentration and began walking backwards with the petrol mower, dreaming perhaps of what to preach on the following Sunday (or more likely, what were we having to eat for our main meal that day!) when I promptly collided with the bank behind me and the mower caught up with my foot. My right foot went numb and soon I noticed my grey socks slowly but surely turning a crimson red! The hospital casualty doctor, upon examining me, comforted me by declaring that I had been fortunate not to have had the tops of all my toes ripped off! As it was, I could not put any weight on my foot for several weeks and was reduced to hopping around like a wounded frog! Thus the Celebration Event in Cardiff by the Province passed me by. Here was another lesson learned. Never look *backward* when looking *forward* achieves the aim without hurting you.

Pontarddulais has a long musical tradition. For many years the Choral Society was a feature of the locality that was much acclaimed; the Pontarddulais Male Voice choir has a reputation second to none in the concert halls of Wales. It was a great privilege for me to invite another Male Voice Choir to the parish on two occasions during my incumbency, namely, Côr Meibion Pontypridd. One of their contingent was my brother, Wayne, who is now one of the most long-standing choristers still singing with them. They provided a feast of music and after their concerts in St. Michael's church, were guests of the Pontarddulais Rugby Club where there was a great spirit of conviviality midst some "impromptu" singing shared with the "rugby boys". Pontypridd Male Voice also came to entertain us later in the parish of Felinfoel, again fraternising with the locals after the concert. It was very generous of the choir to come from such a distance to sing free of charge and assist us with our fund raising. It was no doubt a change for some of the "Bont" choir to sit back and listen to a choir whom many had not had the pleasure of listening to before "on stage" as it were.

In the spring of 1982 we had the Falklands War. Like many parishes, our congregations suddenly increased as families, worried about their loved ones and those of friends, came to share their anxieties with us in church and offer prayers for their safety. Deep down, most people want to cling to a belief in some divine power that rules our lives and, in times of adversity, this desire comes to the surface. Sadly, after the Falklands War was over numbers attending church returned to their usual numbers. Is it too cynical to wish that the Almighty were not treated as though He were a water tap that can be turned on only when we need to fill the kettle and enjoy a strong cup of tea, only to forget about Him when the crisis passes? Perhaps we should be grateful that we remember where the tap is!

My little mishap with the lawnmower was as nothing compared with the constant concern we were having for Sheila's deteriorating health as each year passed. She had been a sufferer from asthma in her childhood but had been mercifully free from it until the Diocesan Parsonage Board, bless them, decided to take down some ceilings of the old "lathe and plaster" kind about a year after we moved into the vicarage. The dust and debris this work caused was monumental. We should have been offered alternative temporary accommodation of course and I should have insisted on this. Sadly this domestic upheaval prompted the asthma to flare up again with a vengeance. In no time her condition became chronic. She was placed in the care of the chest doctor at St. Luke's Hospital for the Clergy and their Dependents in London and the asthma consultant at Singleton hospital in Swansea.

She had to have recourse to a nebuliser and in one or two of the more severe attacks at home was given injections of morphine to relieve the acute shortage of breath. In 1981, after struggling for some time to keep abreast with her teaching duties, she was forced to give up work. Finally the doctor at Singleton advised us to relocate to a higher ground level than that of a river estuary. It was then that I was persuaded that we would soon have to look for another parish. Why these Parsonage Boards do not see fit to make all *essential* repairs before the vicar and family move in amazes me. My successor in the parish was made to move in for a year before a more viable house came on the market down the lane which is the present vicarage. Sometimes the Church moves in very mysterious ways and not always with the well-being of its clergy and their families in mind.

Realising our difficulties, Bishop Vaughan tried his best to keep me batting for his diocesan side. The problem was that the diocese was fairly well staffed at that time. Only two parishes were soon to require incumbents, one was in the Brecon Beacons National Park and the other was in the heart of the city of Swansea. Neither the remoteness of the countryside (however high above sea level) nor the streets of a city appealed to us, so reluctantly we had to look outside the diocese. We finally set our sights on the parish of Aberdare, St. Fagan, situated at the top of the Cynon valley, some three miles from the Heads of the Valleys road leading from Neath to Merthyr Tydfil. We would be back in the diocese of Llandaff now under the fatherly care of Bishop John Poole-Hughes. Ironically in August 1982 my mother, Edith, died quite suddenly after a short illness at the comparatively young age of sixty eight. By the time I had to decide whether to accept the Diocesan Patronage's nomination to the parish at Aberdare it was November of that same year. I felt I was being called to move to where I could visit my father a little more easily, (his home being twelve miles away) since he was prone to severe bronchial attacks. So it was that in March 1983 we were packing our belongings and, like Abraham of old, set about moving tent to the heights of the Glamorgan uplands. For very personal reasons we were leaving the Diocese of Swansea and Brecon, having made many friends and enjoyed a wide range of experiences among the people of Pontarddulais and in the Diocese as a whole. I had been given a thorough insight into managing a truly bilingual parish with added responsibility of being a Rural Dean (the youngest to be appointed in Wales at the time, so I was told) so that I had received useful experience of life beyond the parish boundary and in a diocese in which I felt completely at home. Yet the reality of a serious health problem was an issue that had to come first. It was with some reluctance therefore that we were about to be launched into my second incumbency.

CHAPTER 7

BACK TO THE VALLEYS

We should have taken up residence in Aberdare in February 1983 but the weather in January of that year was so wintry and Sheila's asthma so severe that we were given leave to delay the move until March. What a baptism of fire the start of my ministry turned out to be! Since "the powers that be" were anxious for me to be in post in time for Easter, we had the prospect of the heavy schedule of Holy Week services the week after moving in

St. Fagan's church, Trecynon, Aberdare

and, to crown the week, the stint of my having to take the Three Hours Devotional Service on Good Friday, as nobody had seen fit to arrange for a cleric to take this beforehand. It was convenient that I should see the potential strength of the parish on Easter Day, meeting all three congregations by way of mutual introduction. Nevertheless it was all a little hectic, to say the least.

The parish of Aberdare, St. Fagan consisted of three churches (a) St. Luke's, Cwmdare, a former mining village on the western side of the valley which grew around the Bwllfa Dare colliery, now closed for some time. A recent addition to the local scene had been the opening of the Cwmdare Country Park along the Dare valley which joins the river Cynon in Aberdare (b) the parish church of St. Fagan which dominates the village of Trecynon with the vicarage adjoining the church and its churchyard and (c) the church of St. James in Llwydcoed (referred to by the locals as the "Red Church" because of its red brick structure). Llwydcoed is a residential area on the way from Aberdare to Merthyr Tydfil before the road climbs to meet the Heads of the Valley road. A winding country road from Llwydcoed village takes you to the Llwydcoed Crematorium.

Here then were three distinct communities with the vicar residing right in the middle. Before our arrival, the parish consisted of four churches, the fourth being in Penywaun further up the valley. Mercifully, this church was joined to the neighbouring parish of Hirwaun before my appointment was made. Up until two years before, the parish had always had the services of an assistant priest. The curate's house was still in the possession of the parish but there was little hope of obtaining another curate. Each of the three villages was quite populous, especially when you included the recently built housing estate at Landare, which was nominally part of Cwmdare. So ideally, there was plenty of scope for another priest working with the vicar, even though the parish had been reduced from four to three churches. In fact this parish was to prove to be the sternest test of my ministry and would offer a worthy challenge for me to fulfil my old school motto, "Ymdrech a lwydda" ("Perseverance will succeed").

The amazing thing about being appointed to this parish at all was it contained within its boundary the very school in which I had taught some fifteen years before! In point of fact, one of my first baptisms was that of a child whose father I had taught at Aberdare Boys' Grammar school. Is this perhaps a unique statistic – the fact that I had acted both as teacher and vicar to the father of a child whom I had baptised? Another strange fact was that one of our sidesmen at St. James's was a former pupil of mine and yet another worshipper at the same church was a former colleague on the staff! *"God moves in a mysterious way his wonders to perform."*

The vicarage itself, built in 1858, was quite a manageable and pleasant house except for a rather cumbersome rear access of a stone flight of steps leading from the kitchen to the back garden. A strange feature was the inclusion of the coalhouse *inside* the back door! This was convenient in bad weather but proved to be a double – edged blessing when damp rot set in a year or so after we moved in, prior to the coal being removed when a full gas system was installed. The garden was quite substantial with adequate space for a large lawn, a vegetable plot and flower beds. We grew three rows of runner beans while we were there! Plenty to do therefore to occupy enthusiastic gardeners, but not, however, as daunting as the grounds at Pontarddulais. Two fields adjoining the garden were used for grazing animals so as to give an almost rustic quality to the spot midst the industrial scars of the past. In fact I remember welcoming a group of children with their teachers from a church school in Cardiff and the children were fascinated to watch the sheep and pigs grazing. They had never seen those animals in the flesh before, only on T.V.

St. Luke's had its own church hall to the rear of the church but St. James's had no church hall. St. Fagan's still retained a former church school building which was now in a very sorry state of disrepair but still used by the parish. There is no doubt that its use would have been in blatant disregard of the Health and Safety regulations that apply to premises today. The hazardous condition of this school building and the urgent need of a church hall to take its place was to take up most of my attention for the next two years. Meanwhile I had to face a more pressing problem than this, namely, the state of the pipe organ at the parish church!

The organ had been in the hands of a local "dabbler" in organ renovations who had made a mess of things and left the parish "high and dry" with the job undone and the parish without the benefit of a written contract binding him to its completion to the parish's complete satisfaction. We were left with an instrument which was just about playable, but only just! What was to be done? Fortunately I knew a very competent organ tuner-builder from the Swansea area, Mr Patrick Burns, who had maintained our organ at Pontarddulais. I asked him to come and see what he could make of the situation. He advised us as to what was needed to be done to bring the organ back to full throttle. It meant further expense but it was a case of needs must! It was the only pipe organ in the parish, the other churches having electric organs. A pipe organ requires skilled care and maintenance but its unique sound is quite incomparable. Despite some opposition to spending more on the organ, I convinced members of the P.C.C. that a parish church deserved as good an instrument as we could make it. Within six months the organ was heard in all its glory again. The point is - there should have been a written agreement so that any contingency situation could have been addressed. Having sorted out the organ, we could give full attention to the provision of a church hall.

The first and obvious step was the demolition of the old school – a two-storey building that was such a drain on our resources in terms of insurance and maintenance. One feature of the building was a stone tablet set in the wall above its entrance which said, *"Duw, Cariad yw." ("God is Love")*. We had this tablet removed and stored carefully, ready to be placed in the foyer of the new building where it stands to this day. It was a suitable reminder that God's Love permeates and inspires all our efforts to promote the well-being of the parish. After many site visits from architects, planning officers and clerks of the works, we finally saw the light at the end of the tunnel. We were fortunate in obtaining a grant from the County's Community Projects Scheme and a grant from the Welsh Church Fund. Thus after much fund-raising and tiresome last-minute setbacks such as discovering that the toilets had to be transferred to the other side of the main hall for ease of plumbing arrangements, we were able to arrange for its official opening by Bishop Roy Davies on October 27th.1986. During the opening ceremony St. Fagan's church choir sang a parody of the familiar Harvest hymn, *"Come, ye thankful people, come"* with words that were relevant to the preparations involved towards the "big day".

They went something like:

> *"Come, you lucky people, come*
> *Now the church hall work is done,*
> *Headaches over, worries past,*
> *Building new we have at last"* etc.

(Unfortunately, I have a weakness for trying to compose parodies of hymns, as the need arises!)

The church hall preparations had taken up a lot of my time as it did those who assisted by fund-raising towards the provision of furnishings etc. Nevertheless we now had a facility that met the needs of children's activities, group meetings and provided the opportunity for general outreach to the community - things that are vital towards building up the life of the parish as a supplement to church worship.

Believe it or not, the church hall at St. Fagan's was not my sole pre-occupation during those first two years. As mentioned already, we had a curate's house to be disposed of since I had been given to understand that we could no longer contemplate the possibility of a curate coming. Besides which, our finances had been strained too greatly to afford a curate's expenses of office. To my consternation I discovered that the curate's house was a leasehold property with just twelve years to the lease's expiry. What hope was there of finding a buyer in such a situation? After months of waiting for the estate agent to provide a buyer, I lost patience and set about finding one myself. Finally, to our great relief we found one but at the cost of selling at a price substantially lower than the value of the property. Still, beggars can't be choosers! The estate agents still charged the normal rate for their "expenses". By the end of the two years, I was beginning to think that perhaps I was being called to be a "church plant supremo" rather than the parish priest that I was instituted by Bishop John Poole-Hughes to be.

Such was the stress and strain for that initial period in the parish when it was "all hands on deck", that my own health began to play up. Sheila's asthma condition by now had greatly improved, bearing out the consultant's recommendation to move to higher territory. She hardly needed her nebuliser at all now and, even in the most trying variations of tempera-ture that normally would have brought on attacks, the problem remained under control, apart from the isolated attack. This was one great plus and a great burden off our shoulders. She was even able to see to her beloved greenhouse plants and tend the flower beds which was a joy and delight for her. I always admired her gift for remembering the proper Latin names for plants. To me an "antirrhinum" was a "snap dragon", but she could rattle the names off effortlessly. Her father had kept a large garden at Sully where she had grown up, and, just as I learned some tricks of the trade about growing vegetables from my own father, so she had learned to familiarise herself with the names of flowers from hers.

Meanwhile, ironically, the one whose health was now under scrutiny was me. The crunch came when we returned in August 1983 from a holiday in Devon only for me to feel as fatigued and "washed out" as before we went. After the G.P. admitted me to hospital for tests it was finally established that I had a kidney problem. Apparently I had acquired a "flap" (the term used by the consultant) which had grown over the right kidney, stifling its ability to function properly. Hence the constant fatigue! The surgeon declared that my case was a rare phenomenon for a person of my age. It was normally symptomatic of a child of about ten! I told him that I had been called a late developer by Fr. Bruce of the University Chaplaincy when I told Fr. Bruce that after some years of teaching I had decided to seek ordination!

I was operated on successfully in January 1984 at Prince Charles hospital, Merthyr, but had been on part-duty for a few weeks before admission and about six weeks after returning home. I already had the assistance of a retired priest, the Revd. J.R. Davies, a native of Llanelli, who regularly offered a monthly duty service to provide me with one slightly easier Sunday schedule. He and my good friend, Revd. Douglas Mainwaring, between them, covered for services during my incapacity. Another who assisted as an ordinand gaining parish experience was Bryan Witt, who was later to join me as a colleague in the same deanery in another diocese.

J.R. as everyone called him, was already nearing his eightieth year but was still strong in body and mind and always eager to lend a hand throughout my ministry at Aberdare. Before his retirement he had been

Vicar of Aberpergwm, now the parish of the Vale of Neath. Without his help each month and the occasional services rendered by Doug Mainwaring, whenever Doug's health allowed, I would have been hard pressed to stand up to the pressure. I finally resumed duties on Ash Wednesday 1984. How much debt we owe to the kind services of our retired clergy. This is even more true today with the reduction in manpower (or should I say, "personpower"). No! Let us be even more politically correct and say, "human resources in ministry"! This dependence on the retired clergy is not confined to the situation where a parish is vacant or when a parish priest requires a holiday but in the week by week managing of a busy parish.

Certain wedding occasions come to mind for various reasons. About three weeks into my incumbency I was faced with the daunting prospect of three weddings on the same day, arranged by my predecessor. Personally I had never consented to more than two weddings on the same day. I have to admit that by the third wedding at 3 p.m. I was hard put to walk down the aisle unaided without leading the bride and her father down the aisle. During the wedding promises my mental fatigue was laid bare. I asked the groom, *"Will you have this woman to be your husband, to have and to hold?" etc.* Since the groom was a solicitor's clerk with a sharp eye to things legal, he stared at me coldly and then, in an instant, his face wore a broad grin and he started to giggle. The whole congregation then caught the humour caused by the blunder and all tension that may have been in the air gave way to a riot of laughter. How pleasant it is to laugh at oneself! I got it right the second time, mind!

The second occasion was a double wedding at St. Fagan's in which twin sisters were to be married at the same ceremony. They were the daughters of a local business man and their names were Jayne and Julie. What made the tricky situation more problematic was that the two girls were just about identical and, wonder of wonders, the grooms' names were Iwan and Ieuan! At the wedding rehearsal I teased the couples that they should wear labels with their names on! Imagine my surprise, therefore, when on the day itself they took me at my word and were wearing labels! After we went into the vestry afterwards to sign the registers they informed me that, now that the deed was done, they were abandoning the labels. I am convinced to this day that their thoughtfulness was not just for my peace of mind but theirs, in case both wives ended up with the wrong husbands!

The third occasion was a Blessing of a Civil Marriage Ceremony at St. Fagan's. These services were not that common then. Such an occasion was a "low-key" affair in which the married couple renewed their promises and vows in the presence of their close relatives and friends without the elaborate arrangements of a full Marriage Service. Unfortunately, I forgot to check my diary that week and, assuming that I had the Saturday afternoon free, started to do a spot of gardening. At about 2 p.m. I espied a group of well-dressed people doing a tour of the church grounds as though they were preparing to attend a big occasion. The truth dawned, as I recognised some of the faces. I had forgotten I had the Blessing Ceremony. In a panic I shot upstairs to take off my "glad rags" and put on my suit and collar, went over to open the church and apologising

(God forgive me!) for forgetting that the service was fixed for 2 p.m. and not 2.30 p.m.! I just could not bring myself to risk their thinking that I thought so little of the occasion as to forget all about it. What a blessing that the house was adjacent to the church and that Sheila and I had not gone off to do some shopping! I am not a great devotee of having to live next door to the church as it can be too convenient for people to call for the key when you are enjoying some time off. A parish priest and his/her family need some space to themselves. But it can be useful to live "on the premises" in emergencies like the occasion when the Blessing nearly did not take place!

The fact that Sheila was now released from teaching and enjoying better health allowed her time to "do her own thing" more easily. Besides the church choir at St. Fagan's and flower arranging when called upon by those not as gifted in that direction, she decided to join a mixed choir in Trecynon. This was the Ebenezer Choral Society, which originally was a choir whose members were limited to a Welsh chapel, but now membership was open to anyone. In fact it was the oldest chapel choir still functioning in the whole of the valleys, if not in South Wales. I decided to join as well, as they were desperate, naturally, for male voices. We found the experience refreshing because both of us enjoyed music and being in this choir enabled us to be free from the status of vicar and vicar's wife, simply enjoying the fellowship for its own sake. When the able conductor, Eirlys Hatton, was taken ill for a while, Sheila was asked to "fill in" at rehearsals. She enjoyed it as much as they appreciated her help. We sang oratorio work such as Mendelssohn's "Elijah" and Haydn's

"Creation" together with many songs in Welsh, both traditional and modern.

The Aberdare area always had a strong tradition of keeping the Welsh language alive, especially in Non-conformist circles. There was a strong Aberdare Cymrodorion Society which promoted activities and fellowship all of which was conducted in Welsh. The parish held a monthly Communion service in Welsh at St. Fagan's to which about a dozen or so came faithfully. The deeds of the land on which St. Fagan's church was built stated that *"while the river Cynon flows, the Welsh language will be retained in this church."* I am pleased to say that this legal condition is still being complied with today. There was a small Welsh congregation at St. John Baptist church in the town parish of Aberdare. With the agreement of the then Vicar, Archdeacon Gordon James, we held a combined Welsh Evensong each quarter in alternate churches, notwithstanding a Harvest Festival and Advent Carols. Bishop Roy came as our preacher on one occasion. Since he was a fluent Welsh speaker, he was glad to have the opportunity of sharing in an all-Welsh service as a change from the medium of English, which predominated in the Diocese of Llandaff at large. There are still pockets of the Welsh language in a number of parishes in the diocese, particularly in the Archdeaconry of Margam. It seems to me that such a situation calls for us to look at "the big picture" and arrange "area services" wherever travel to the churches within any given area is convenient. Each year there is still a Welsh Festival at Llandaff Cathedral which draws Welsh speakers together for a "Big Sing". I cannot see why each fifth Sunday, for instance, such a pattern cannot but bring a greater fellowship to the scattered, possibly frustrated, small congregations in the parts of our Province where English is the dominant language. It may indeed help to promote a greater sensitivity towards the Welsh language among clergy and lay people in such parishes whose confidence in Welsh needs a boost.

Sadly there was not much scope for ecumenical activity in Aberdare, St. Fagan, since, unlike Pontarddulais, there was only one resident Non-conformist minister to work with. He was the redoubtable Revd D.O.Davies, a Welsh Baptist minister whose church was located in Cwmdare. We had very friendly relations and shared Harvest and Carol services each year. Despite his advanced age he was a vigorous character and was well known and respected in the area, having ministered in the community for nearly 40 years! It was a privilege to be present at his dear wife, Lois's, death bed during the period when I myself was a hospital patient. They were both true servants of the Gospel.

Sheila found another outlet for her talents by arranging trips of all kinds to places of interest not only for the choristers to join other choirs for special "Sing Ins" but also excursions that were open to all and sundry. One trip was to the Cider Works at Hereford, followed by a guided tour of the cathedral. Visits to "Pick-your-Own Fruit venues were very popular. She delighted in arranging the day in such a way as to cater for options for those who wanted to pursue their own activities rather than "following the throng."

I suppose that for every parish priest there stands out a certain character remembered for his or her distinctive sayings. Such a character that always comes to my mind when I think of Trecynon is Ethel Jones. Ethel was almost ninety when I first met her. Her father had sold cockles picked at Penclawdd and, as a girl, she was his assistant. Whenever I called, she would always be sitting in the same armchair in the living room beside a roaring coal fire in an old-fashioned black-lead grate, the same huge fire, be it summer or winter. Her reminiscences of life of former days was remarkable. There was not one visit that I made on her when she did not return to her favourite saying. *"Do you know, vicar,"* she would begin, *"every day I live, my ship is travelling that much nearer to my harbour of safety."* She would then ask me, *"Have I mentioned this to you before?"* To which I lied, *"No, Mrs Jones, and it's a lovely picture you paint!"* Of course, I had heard her say those words dozens of times, but how could I spoil her delight in sharing this lovely image of the Christian pilgrim with me by telling the truth? May she, with all the faithful, rest for ever in the eternal haven where they would be!

In 1984 a special Oberammergau Passion Play was staged to commemorate the anniversary of the start of the annual event in Germany (the Play is normally held to mark the start of the decade). I took twenty two parishioners, linking up with a further eighteen in London for the journey to Austria where we stayed for eight days, I being responsible for all forty in the party. This was only a few months after recuperating from my operation, of course, so I was not quite as lively, physically, as I would have wished. Seeing the Passion Play was a very moving experience, the music being as riveting as the acting. The fact that the performance was in German did nothing to detract from the enjoyment. In fact it added a new dimension to such a familiar text.

Due to its size, the parish had a wide variety of points of contact. Each of the three villages had its primary school; we also had a comprehensive school, a College of Further Education, a geriatric hospital and even, (when all else failed!) a crematorium at Llwydcoed! There were also four residential homes and one nursing home. Just outside the parish boundary was the diocesan high school of St. John Baptist, one of only three such high schools in the diocese, the other two being located in Cardiff (I had taught in one of them - the Bishop of Llandaff School). The close proximity of St. John Baptist School meant that parents with close (or tenuous) links with the Church were anxious for their children to be prepared for Confirmation in order to secure a place for them in the school. Since pupils had to be baptised *and* confirmed in order to be eligible for a place, my Confirmation classes for young people were much larger than I was used to. This was splendid as regards their being instructed in the Faith as a platform for living a Christian life, but in view of the fact that, after their Confirmation, most of them were seldom seen in church, it would seem to have been a "paper exercise" on the part of the parents and the school – unless one is gratified that the pupils are influenced for good by compulsory attendance at a school Eucharist. Most of us as clergy know what it is like to be disillusioned by the falling away in attendance at church of young people after Confirmation. But in this particular situation, the problem was made more acute by the distinct possibility that the desire to be confirmed came from the parents more than from the young people themselves. As it is, I have great reservations about seeing, *at parish level,* a great many children of ten or eleven years of age being possibly pressurised into being communicants of the Church just to satisfy the requirements of a church school admission policy. At the same time, children of a non-Anglican family who worship regularly at, say, a Roman Catholic or Wesleyan Methodist church, are refused entry to that school because of their non-Anglican status? Are not the *Christian ethos and shared values within an Anglican context* the crux of the matter here, especially in these days when inclusiveness is, rightly, so greatly prized by society as a whole? The long tradition of Church Education in the Aberdare area accounted for one of its schools, Mardy House, being used during the World War 2 years as temporary accommodation for St. Michael's College to offset the dire threat from bombing. (Llandaff Cathedral was badly damaged in 1940)

In 1986 we had to arrange for Sheila's mother, who was a widow, to come and live with us. She had been getting increasingly frail over recent years and we found it so difficult to get to her home in Sully to see to things because of the distance involved. We converted my study downstairs into a bedroom for her and transferred the study upstairs. She had her little walk most days down the lane to post her letters to family and friends (she was an inveterate letter writer). However, slowly her condition worsened and she died peacefully after a short period in hospital in 1988. At least we had made her last days on this earth a little more comfortable and afforded her some needed company at the end of life's journey.

The "cottage" hospital at Fedw Hir was accessed via a winding country road above the village of Llwydcoed - a quiet, secluded spot. I went each month to give the patients Communion. This was the only hospital that I was ever to minister to as the parish priest. I was visibly impressed by the number of visitors who came to see their elderly relatives on the first Christmas Eve that I was there. My pleasant reaction turned to disillusion when the matron confided in me:- *"Sad to say, vicar, but this will be the last I will see of most of these visitors until next Christmas, apart from birthdays during the year."* Why do some people make a supreme effort to be thoughtful at a festive time but are conspicuous by their thoughtlessness for the rest of the time? Perhaps it is a case of "guilty conscience"? Maybe, after all, once or twice is better than never!

In 1987 we held a memorable series of events to celebrate the centenary of St. Luke's. Apart from Bishop Roy being our celebrant on the Feast of Dedication itself, in company with Archdeacon John Lewis, a good friend of the church at Cwmdare over the years, the service was followed by a splendid lunch in the church hall. We were able to welcome clergy who had previously served in the parish as guest preachers during the year, such as Canon Dennis Parry, who had moved to the diocese of Bangor and the Very Revd. Brian Henry, then Dean of Cyprus. Among other events we had a most enjoyable day in Bath and Wells, ending with Evensong at Wells, one of my favourite cathedrals. I like it not only because of its famous, magnificent west window but because of its unique setting, complete with swans around its perimeter. We received a warm welcome as a group from the Canon-in-Residence and we were fortunate in having a lovely summer's day. I shall always remember the evening sun streaming through the cathedral windows as we thanked God for the good work of the faithful in past generations and pledged ourselves to pass on our heritage to those who would come after us. Truly an atmosphere to inspire us on our Christian pilgrimage through life.

It was a great privilege for me to accept an invitation from my successor in the parish to preach at the centenary service of St. James's, Llwydcoed, in 1998. Seeing friends again there at another parish centenary event was an uplifting experience. Celebrations like these are a constant reminder to us, as Christians, that we live in a time capsule in which we live for the present, are mindful of our heritage in the past but with eyes firmly focused on what lies ahead of us.

Aberdare, St. Fagan, was the first parish in which I had the pleasure of commending a person offering himself for training for Holy Orders. This was Martyn Gough. He and his family were faithful members of St. Luke's. Martyn was just twenty when he first confided in me his thoughts about vocation to the sacred ministry. Bearing in mind his youthfulness, I advised him to explore the possibility of pursuing voluntary work with the Missions to Seafarers as a way of gaining valuable experience working with others in the name of the Church as he would not be able to start formal training until he was twenty two. After a fruitful stint assisting the chaplain in the port of Rotterdam in Holland, Martyn never looked back after ordination and has spent the majority of his ministry as a chaplain in the Royal Navy.

During the mid 1980's the Diocesan Director of Education asked me to resume my school inspection work. The system had changed a little over the past decade. Instead of an approach whereby the Inspector quizzed the class in the style of a Grand Inquisitor, he now observed the teacher at work and resorted to asking questions of pupils in a more "low-key" fashion while pupils were on task. This was a far more positive approach. The whole essence of teaching Religious Education revolves around subtle questioning. Often the question "Why?" digs deeper than the questions, "How?" or "Where?" or "When?" and questioning an individual pupil or a small group of pupils produces more satisfying results in this respect. The few weeks in the Summer Term when the inspectors were allotted their schools for inspection turned out to be a welcome "break" from the pastoral demands of parish routine for me. They say that a change of scene is as good as a rest.

I have to say that, as with Roy and Ray in the parish in the Rhondda, I had two excellent "men about the church" in Gus Jenkins and Len Preece, who were always ready to be of service whenever there was a need for minor repairs etc. You name it and they were both willing and very able to "do the honours" without any fuss or claim for credit. Sadly, a few years after I left the parish Len suffered a major stroke which greatly diminished his quality of life. We were fortunate in having such capable helpers.

Russell Bound was another layman who not only faithfully assisted at the altar in worship but did lots of work behind the scenes to lighten my load.

In 1984 we engaged the services of the Government organisation known as the Manpower Services. Commission to do a "blitz" on St. Fagan's churchyard. Local Authorities were empowered to engage them to undertake appropriate community projects free of labour charge. Ours was an awkward churchyard with a steep slope at one end and undulating levels of ground elsewhere. The aim was to realign headstones that had gone askew or toppled over, dispose of unwanted kerbstones, and remove the more elaborate features that marked Victorian attitudes to burial such as iron chains around the grave and tall obelisks. Much of the concentration of the Victorian mind on grief at death led to some quite hideous and quite unchristian manifestations of the soul imprisoned. To remove the most overt of these seemed a boost for the positive message of life through the power of the Risen Lord. Before the Manpower "boys" could begin their renovations, we had to record for posterity the inscriptions on each grave – a fairly weighty task for volunteers. We split into small groups taking a corner of the churchyard each. Actually we benefitted from sharing stories about the sad cases of infant mortality, the tragic causes of death through typhoid, colliery accidents etc. or people buried there whose descendants were known to us. We were given an "on site" snapshot of the social history of the parish during those few months that we were recording those inscriptions. As a result of our efforts we had an updated plan of the churchyard and a more attractive, easier to maintain and safer environment for the visitor and those responsible for the care of the churchyard.

Churchyards can be a headache for clergy and churchwardens. There are so many rules and regulations attached to their maintenance that have to be implemented and relationships with grave owners (especially those with no formal links to the Church) can be fraught at times. Yet churchyards tell a story – of the transitory nature of this mortal life, yes, but also that we are called to be pilgrims of the "hope eternal" during our lives on earth. They also remind us as we stroll among them of the priority of *people* and the privilege of serving them at every stage in life which we as clergy inherit by our privileged calling.

We had some hilarious Harvest Suppers in the parish. There is something special about a "home-spun" Harvest supper with talent on tap as presented by the parishioners themselves. I remember us having great fun and the audience having a riotous time as three "gendarmes" dressed to kill offered a unique rendering of the familiar Gilbert and Sullivan song "*We're on the run*". One of the three was the tall figure of a real Chief Superintendent of Police, namely John Welford, another was the diminutive figure of Russell Bound and between the two extremes was yours truly.

It brought the house down but did nothing I'm afraid, to bring the crime rate down!

Despite these and many other causes for enjoyment and good relationships with parishioners, I was beginning to get somewhat desperate for some form of help in ministry in order to "keep the machine going", let alone be able to venture in mission in the parish. As regards the maintenance of services I did have the assistance of a Licensed Reader, Edwin Brace, but Edwin was committed to playing the organ at St. James's; besides which it was help with the number of Eucharists that was needed the most. The Bishop was supportive of my difficulties and informed me that a Lay Worker was a possibility. One such person was found but she lived on the outskirts of Cardiff and could not drive so this was not a practical proposition. Meanwhile a friend of mine told me in confidence (these things often occur in such a small Province as Wales) that a parish in the Llanelli area was vacant with just one church, a strong Sunday congregation, a good choral tradition, a large Sunday School and a licensed Lay Reader. The Bishop of St.Davids, Archbishop George Noakes, must have heard of a possible interest on my part and telephoned to say that he was particularly interested in my being able to take on a role in the field of education in the Diocese and the role had to be filled, ideally, by a person able to speak Welsh. It sounded attractive. Sheila and I went to have a look around. We saw a comfortably sized church, holding about 250 people, a pleasant, if large, vicarage with rather daunting grounds which almost put us off the whole idea! Still we can all wear rose-tinted spectacles at times. To combat this we gained the impression from the Rural Dean, Canon John Byron Davies, that the area was a friendly environment in which to work and that people would respond to the right kind of leadership. I then had a constructive meeting with Bishop Roy, in stark contrast with the meeting with my bishop when I was about to leave the diocese of Llandaff in 1975. Being a native of the Llanelli area himself, the bishop could confirm the bilingual nature and industrial background of Llanelli, thus understanding my capacity to "fit in" to the scene without difficulty. As Bishop Roy sanguinely put it, *"After all, Alan, we are all working for the same firm in the end."* I had the distinct feeling that, despite losing a priest from the diocese of Llandaff, the bishop knew that such an area of South Wales would use such gifts as I could offer more widely with less onerous demands on my energy.

The move was decided upon. Again it would be a move motivated for very personal reasons. The pressure of maintaining three quite busy and diverse churches, dealing with so many funerals, christenings and weddings among such a populous area was blunting my appetite for tackling the challenge of sharing the Gospel in the spirit of mission in the community. In the parish of St. Fagan circumstances had forced me to take on the role of" crisis management" supervisor to a far greater extent than I would have wished. I needed to focus on a situation in which parish management could be balanced more equitably with the pastoral role which clergy (at least in my time!) were trained to undertake. We had the satisfaction, at least, of leaving the parish in a much healthier state than when we arrived. We were ready now to look west once more, but beyond the River Loughor, to a new diocese and new challenges, never to return to parish ministry in the diocese that nurtured Sheila and myself in the Faith.

CHAPTER 8

THE OTHER SIDE
OF THE LOUGHOR

Having so far tasted life to the east of the river Loughor we were now moving to the coastal town of Llanelli in Carmarthenshire, some five miles west of the Loughor which is the boundary between the county of Swansea and Carmarthenshire. The parish of Felinfoel, with its church dedicated to the Holy Trinity, stands

Holy Trinity church, Felinfoel, Llanelli

about a mile to the north of the town along the bank of the little river Lliedi as it makes its way to the estuary in North Dock, Llanelli. At my Institution service in January 1989, Bishop Ivor Rees, who was Assistant Bishop to Archbishop Noakes, welcomed Sheila and myself by saying, *"You have now crossed the river Jordan and landed safely in the Land of Promise."* Certainly I was to feel within a short space of time a noticeably different "feel" about the Land of Promise as opposed to places in which we had hitherto resided as pilgrims. Looking at the diocese geographically, it was a much more rural diocese, obviously. However, we were making our home near a town known for its urban ambience. The eastern part of Carmarthenshire from the top of the Amman valley down through the Gwendraeth valley to Cydweli, with its two large towns of Ammanford and Llanelli contains the largest density of population in the county and bears all the hallmarks of a vibrant industrial past. "Pottery Street" and "Copper Works Road" in Llanelli speak for themselves in this respect. In fact the close-knit community lifestyle and the cultural elements of love of music and rugby can be favourably compared with features of the valleys, so familiar to me. I often admit that Llanelli could very well be considered a "grand valley town by the sea"– with its terraced houses, industrial scars and steep gradients to test the breath control! Yes! – We were stepping into "foreign soil" but in a way it was a case of "déjà vu" - with a slight difference.

The parish church of Llanelli, dedicated to St. Elli, lies in the middle of the town and is an ancient Celtic site, though the oldest part of the present building is the tower with its six bells, dating from the 12th century.

Holy Trinity Church, Felinfoel, is an attractive building of cruciform design with its copper spire crowning the centre–piece of the cross. The church was founded as one of several chapels-of-ease to St. Elli's and was consecrated by Bishop Thirlwall on Trinity Sunday, 1858. The benefactors were the Nevill family, Richard Nevill being an industrialist from Birmingham who had opened a substantial copper works in the town in 1805. During the following decades his industrial empire expanded and, with it, the Nevill's concern for the spiritual well-being of their employees. Originally the church spire was made of traditional stone but in the 1960's a new spire of green copper replaced it to represent the link with the copper industry associated with its benefactors. A church school was erected on the east side of the church in the 1870's, again through the generosity of Richard Nevill. This school closed in 1969, its former pupils being encouraged to attend the new Swiss Valley county primary school that had just been built to provide for the growing number of children on the new housing estate to the north of the village. There has always been a close affinity between the parish and this school, the vicar being a welcomed, regular visitor to school assembly, which is also true of the Felinfoel Primary School in the village itself. The old church school building, consisting of three large classrooms, was converted into the Church Hall and was extended in 1977 to accommodate an extra "games room". It was here that the celebrated one time world champion snooker player Terry Griffiths learned his trade on the professional table that was kept in this room. In 1882 the mission church at Graiglwyd was built to serve the farming population between the road to Llannon and the hamlet of Porth Dafen to the east. This "little church on the rock", as it was called locally, closed in 1962. With the advent of the car this church, like many another mission church in rural areas, suffered the fate of being the victim of a more mobile society.

Holy Trinity church remained a chapel-of-ease to the parish church of Llanelli until, with the huge increase in population during the latter part of the nineteenth century, it was decided to grant parish status to Felinfoel in 1887. The Revd. J.W. Roberts was the first incumbent. He and his parishioners must have enjoyed a warm relationship together because he remained until his retirement in 1914.

The site for a vicarage, as opposed to a curate's house which had been located near the church, was provided by the Buckley family who had founded the famous brewery in the village. The site of the vicarage was an acre in size and situated about 300 yards up the road from the church towards Llannon. Like most Victorians of substance, the Buckley family were over-generous in the apportionment of land, leading to much consternation on the part of successive incumbents who struggled to maintain the grounds.

My first Sunday in the parish began on a clear, frosty morning in late January. Despite the cold weather I was greeted by substantial congregations at 8 a.m. 9.30 (Welsh) and 10.45 a.m. Evensong was the big surprise – about 40 present. I was delighted to know that I had the assistance of an able Lay Reader, Hugh Richards, who had the extra qualification of being fluent in Welsh. This was a bonus in a bilingual situation in which a regular service in Welsh was essential.

I was delighted to see about 80 children in Sunday school at the church hall in the afternoon. Of course with the three large rooms available, the classes could be dispersed according to age-groups so that activity could take place in one room without inhibiting others. The Sunday school was truly continuing the tradition of the building, the former church school. There is no doubt that, as I found with the old school in the Trecynon area of Aberdare, the presence of a church school tradition in the parish from days gone by creates a continuing church-going ethos for future generations. The seeds once sown bear fruit. My first Confirmation class of young people in 1990 numbered twenty three and the adult group numbered five. Nowadays the trend is towards more adults than young people. Sadly, many young people fell away from church attendance after Confirmation, yet a good number returned to church life later on as their children were growing up. Teenage years are a time of emotional complexity and often bring to the surface a rebellious spirit. What is the right age for young people to be confirmed? The answer depends on so many things. The strength of their own desire to be confirmed is all important. Pressure of time due to school examinations comes into the equation. I had plenty of encouragement at home which counts for so much, but it was never coercion on the part of my parents. One thing is clear - It is never too late to be confirmed! As a curate in Glyncoch I recall preparing a lady of seventy five for confirmation. At the time she was old enough to be my grandmother. So what? *"My grace is all sufficient"*, says the apostle, Paul, in his second letter to the Corinthians.

The first few months of our settling into parish life were marred by the loss of our terrier/corgi dog, Siân. She had been with us for 14 years since we rescued her from the Dogs' Home (now more kindly called a Canine Rescue Centre) in Swansea. She had been ailing with a kidney problem for some time. I remember one event in Trecynon when we thought we had lost her for good. She had burrowed through the soil in the garden in pursuit of a weasel or some other creature and succeeded in burying herself underground. We could hear a faint yelping noise so we had an idea where she was. We called the Fire Brigade and they got her back to safety, bruised but not beaten! They say, "As tenacious as a terrier" and she certainly lived up to that name. However, on Mothering Sunday 1989 at 4 p.m., her tenacity was at last spent and she had to be put to sleep. We still had our cat, Lucy, who had been bequeathed to us by a friend in Pontarddulais. She gave us a scare too when workmen had placed scaffolding on the vicarage roof which she found so tempting to climb that she would not come back down for four days. Back to ground level at last, she was very dehydrated by this ordeal but lived to "tell the tale", as they say. Lucy and Siân were good friends. Their only "spats" came when one fancied eating the other's food. Usually it was Siân who was the greedy one but Lucy the one who drew the "spat" to a conclusion! Those who say that dog walking is a chore and avoid it as much as possible miss out on making friends, that is, with other dog walkers. Mind you, the dogs get more attention than the dog–owners on these excursions!

Only two fairly minor problems with fabric faced us in Felinfoel and they had to do with the church hall.

The flat roof on the extension needed replacing and a new perimeter fence needed to be erected at the rear of the car park. It was suggested by Sheila and other musically-inclined "conspirators" that we get together a mixed choir and arrange some concerts to help towards fund raising. We called ourselves the Trinity Singers. The aim was to sing a blend of sacred and secular music for formal and more informal occasions. So we would offer Stainer's "Crucifixion" and Maunder's "Olivet to Calvary" or simple church anthems in a church setting while at Harvest Suppers, entertaining Senior Citizen's groups etc. we sang folk songs and items from musicals (including an ambitious stab at a Gilbert and Sullivan chorus from "The Gondoliers"). By 1991 we had not only succeeded in our original aim of easing the financial burden towards the provision of facilities for the church hall but had unanimously decided to carry on singing for the sheer enjoyment. Over the next few years our concerts were well received and we were making our mark as singing troubadours in our part of the diocese and beyond. We even spread our wings as far as the far west of Wales, singing to help promote parish projects in parishes such as Ystrad Aeron and Aberaeron.

Our age range was wide. We had a couple of teenagers from the church choir; we even recruited children to sing solos for Andrew Lloyd Webber's "Pie Iesu" and Cesar Franck's "Panis Angelicus". We also had our own adult solo voices for the popular religious musicals of Roger Jones that had become well known just then, such as "Mary Jones" (based on the story of Mary Jones and her Bible), "Greater than Gold" and "Simeon." There was no maximum age to the membership of the choir. We had a few who were eighty years young.

The two regular hallmarks of the year for the Singers were the Harvest Supper and the Christmas Carol concert. Sheila was particularly fond of Christmas music and would introduce us to less well known carols from far and wide, such as the "Sans Day" carol from Cornwall or "What is this fragrance?" from France, so that we always had a variety in our repertoire. She was also a "dab hand" at composing her own descants which provided some diversity to the performances.

Just like the Songsters which we set up in Pontarddulais, the Trinity Singers provided an outlet for outreach to the community and identifying the Church as an agency which cares essentially for those who are NOT its members, unlike other secular societies. It is pleasing that the Singers continue this outreach today under the competent baton of their former accompanist, Helen Smith, with the versatile Hilda Rees on the piano.

One of the important fund-raising events of the year that we inherited was the Spring Fair in early May. This was a time when planting in the garden went on apace and so the plant stall was a great attraction. There was already a flourishing Gardening Club in the village, which identified the community as essentially a village community. Felinfoel had developed from its beginnings as a village around the mill by the river Lliedi. It then grew, due to the substantial housing estate of Swiss Valley and smaller housing complexes being erected on the edge of the village, to a suburb of Llanelli. Despite this growth in population it retained its "village" ethos and outlook in many ways. I was in conversation with someone near the village post office a few weeks after moving in when suddenly I heard a distant but very audible crash. *"You know what that is, vicar,* said the man to whom I was speaking, *"It's the Westfa House being demolished!"* This was a home once inhabited by some of the Nevill family. It was being taken down to be replaced by a small estate of houses. It is a pity that although one comes across Nevill Street in the town of Llanelli, there is no landmark commemorating the family name in the community which they had done so much to influence. Perhaps Richard's daughter, Blanche, who was a former organist in Holy Trinity church, would have been a suitable choice of name for one of the streets in Felinfoel for that very reason. Blanche and her sister Catherine had done much to establish a musical tradition that is clearly evident today in the life of the parish. So with the demise of Llys Westfa came the end of an era for Felinfoel's landmarks. However, memory of the Nevills as a family still lived on through The Plas Residential Home for the elderly, situated near Adulam chapel. The Plas was originally the home of another branch of the Nevill family. My first visit to the Plas was a memorable one. All the staff and residents gave me a very special welcome. They sang with heart and voice, "We'll keep a welcome in the hillsides" as I arrived. I was truly moved by this gesture and I was always welcomed warmly at the Home thereafter. I am sure that the benefactors of the church who founded it and had lived in this house would have been very gratified that the incumbent of their beloved church had been given such a "red carpet" treatment and that the good people of the area were receiving the kind of care and kindness there of which the Nevills would have approved.

By the time the Spring Fair of 1990 was held, the vicarage garden had contributed quite handsomely towards the plant stall. During our first year we had prepared and begun to cultivate a vegetable plot, a soft fruit area and even the flower beds, rockeries and hanging baskets were beginning to look attractive. By the start of 1990 we had a greenhouse erected, to Sheila's great delight. From then on, she joined forces with Gardening Club secretary, Denzil Adams, who was a faithful sidesman and a willing, useful handyman around the church, to assemble the stall. Orders would come in each year from "regular customers" looking for a bargain! One could rely on the plant stall to bring in proceeds of several hundreds of pounds each year.

If Sheila was the cultivator-in-chief of our garden, I was head grounds man! There was no let up from March to October with regard to keeping everything under some sort of control. Often my official weekly "day off" from parish duties would be taken up with both of us toiling away outdoors. I think I prepared more sermons weeding the garden than poring over bible commentaries in the study.

One rather damp day I rigged up a scarecrow to ward off marauding birds from attacking our bean crop. The scarecrow was decked in an old trilby hat and one of my old mackintoshes. The following day I called on some neighbours whose back garden bordered on the rear wall of the vicarage. The husband whispered in a very solicitous tone, "*Oh! Vicar, we are so relieved that you are out and about. We thought you would surely catch pneumonia out in the garden all day in the rain yesterday. Do have a drop of brandy just to make sure!*" Naturally, to refuse the drink would have been an insult to their concern for me!"

I have great cause to remember one particular day in October 1989. It was the day that the south east of England suffered tremendous destruction from a storm that ravaged the country. South Wales received the tail end of this storm. However even the tail wagged fiercely as I found to my cost. I was just venturing outside to fetch some coal when I heard a loud "crack!" that in seconds became a fearful "crash". The large chestnut tree opposite the front door of the house had been felled by the force of the wind. I just stood still as if caught up in a dream as the huge tree (so beloved by children who used to come and ask if they could collect some conkers in season) buckled and fell, mercifully, away from the house and over the wall dividing our drive from a neighbours' garden, to end up prostrate in that garden. Had the direction of the wind been from the east, the tree would have struck the house, possibly taking me in its wake. I have experienced some hazardous weather in my life – driving in dense fog over the Brecon Beacons being one I would care to forget – but for sheer unexpected drama this was the most alarming incident involving the weather that has ever happened to me. I was sorry for the damage caused to our neighbours' garden but they were the first to admit that this mishap was preferable to a damaged house or an injured clergyman! The children were forced to go elsewhere for their conkers from then on!

I had many a quarrel with the rather ancient "sit-on" petrol mower which we had inherited from previous occupants of the vicarage. It broke down as often as it cut the grass, leaving it stranded with me unable to push it back to its home in the former stable. Yes, stable! It had wooden stalls to house the non-existent horse!

After many repairs and mini crises we gave up on the mower and bought a second-hand one in good condition which was a distinct improvement on the previous one. To be fair, the parish contributed substantially towards the cost. All went well until one day the mower got bogged down in mud at the bottom end of the lawn on a day prior to which we had had heavy rain. The more I revved up the engine, the deeper into the mire I penetrated. Finally I called up the services of the gravedigger and his assistant. Together we manhandled the mower to firmer ground. Can you imagine the local press straining at the leash to publish the eye-catching headline:-"*Vicar rescued from grave situation by gravedigger!*" My name would have been "mud", as they say! In fact there were many underground springs in our garden and even a moderate amount of rain would cause a machine to flounder. I knew I should have passed an advanced driving test on that mower. The soil was so waterlogged at times that many a frog would jump over my spade while I was digging. Once a more brazen creature landed on the edge of the garden fork (I was not using it at the time!) and began croaking. A real Romeo, anxious to find his Juliet!

My church organ problems were not over when I left my previous parish. On my arrival at Felinfoel I found to my consternation an electric organ in use with the original pipe organ "in mothballs" behind it. Apparently a former organist had insisted on the parish investing in a new electric organ of the latest model when it was obvious that the pipe organ needed a lot of money spent on it. As at Trecynon, I nailed my sails firmly to the mast that a parish church deserves the wholesome sound of a pipe organ and that since the organ needed an overhaul, then it must have one, however inconvenient it may be to fund the work. On being informed that it would cost approx. £20,000 to put the organ back into shape, we set up an Organ Renovation Fund. As if in answer to a prayer, within a few months we had notification of a bequest to the church of £15,000 to be spent at the discretion of the vicar and churchwardens. The bequest was part of the estate of Mrs Bronwen Evans, formerly of Felinfoel, but who for many years had lived in the Rhondda. As coincidence would have it, Bronwen had been a faithful worshipper in St. Peter's church, Pentre where I had known her fifteen years before! It was a privilege to officiate at her burial service at Holy Trinity because here was someone who was one of my "flock" in another place but who after the wanderings of this mortal life came to rest in peace where she had begun life's journey. How strange that a previous parishioner of mine should be responsible for coming to the rescue of my present parish, as though Bronwen knew when her generosity was most needed. Our efforts to raise funds, together with the bequest, meant that the work on the pipe organ was duly completed. We donated the electric organ (now superfluous) to Trinity College Chapel, Carmarthen, for the use of students learning to play the organ. One kind gesture deserved a gesture in kind. The pipe organ has played splendidly ever since. I am sure that this would have gladdened the hearts of Catherine and Blanche Nevill, among many others.

It seemed that church music was always destined to play a large part in my activities as a parish priest. As always I supported Sheila's efforts in maintaining standards in the church choir. St. Davids Cathedral was now the venue for the annual R.S.C.M. Festivals with special "Sing in" training sessions for choirs in the Archdeaconry, usually held in St Peter's Church, Carmarthen. I recall a splendid combined Festal Evensong in which the choir of St. Mary's Church, Cydweli, came to join us at Holy Trinity for our Dedication Festival on Trinity Sunday when their vicar, Revd. Graham Davies, later Archdeacon of St. Davids, had been asked to preach. It was a lovely occasion musically; we sang Stanford's "O be joyful in the Lord", a special setting of Psalm 150 and special settings of the Canticles. It was also a great evening of fellowship. Too often we are all so isolated in our own "little patches", often struggling to keep up our numbers (especially at evening worship). Through the choirs uniting, we were able to promote a spirit of unity among the congregations because a good number of "supporters" from St. Mary's came to join us in worship. How I wish I could hear a high standard of choral singing in more churches today. As it is, Evensong has almost died a death as a sung service and, with its fast disappearance as a choral service, we lose those marvellous evening canticles and some glorious evening hymns like *"The day thou gavest, Lord, is ended"* which is often now limited to watching T.V.'s "Songs of Praise".

As regards congregations coming together, we achieved the almost unthinkable in Felinfoel quite early in my ministry there. Twice a year the minister of Adulam and I agreed that the worshippers at Adulam Welsh Baptist chapel and those at Holy Trinity should unite in the Week of Prayer for Christian Unity and during Christian Aid Week in alternate churches. I say "unthinkable" because I had heard stories of days gone by when a Baptist minister would perhaps venture to attend a graveside committal in Holy Trinity churchyard but never think of darkening the doors of the church for service there. Similarly, the vicar would never "humble himself" to take part in a service in the chapel. Those were the days of "them" and "us". Nowadays we take more notice of the Psalmist's words:

"How good and pleasant a thing it is when people live together in unity."

The unfortunate situation today is that there are often insufficient resources in the ordained ministry to build relationships of this kind between denominations. I include Roman Catholic clergy, Non-Conformist clergy and our own Anglican clergy in this regard. For relationships between churches to succeed one must have co-operation, mutual trust and respect between the clergy and ministers involved, which hopefully will then be "caught on" by their congregations.

I have already mentioned the fact that Archbishop Noakes had asked me to take on a diocesan remit as Assistant Director of Education on my appointment to Felinfoel. As soon as I took up this role, The Director himself, who was Head of Religious Studies at Trinity College, Carmarthen, left for Oxford University to do some research for six months. This left me "holding the fort" in a brand new situation and in a diocese with which I was not familiar! This was a far cry from the inspecting role which I had been used to before. Now it was a case of "sink or swim". In 1992 the Director, who is the present Bishop of St. Davids, the Rt. Revd. Wyn Evans, became Dean of St. Davids and Bishop Ivor Rees, who had now become our bishop at the retirement of Archbishop Noakes, appointed me as the new Director of Education. I recall the words of the then Archdeacon of St. Davids, the Ven. John Harvey, in wishing me well, *"Best wishes, Alan, in coping with the bed of nails!"* This had to be an omen of things to come.

Not many people realise that in the diocese of St.Davids there were at that time some forty two church schools, scattered over an area ranging from St. Davids in Pembrokeshire in the west to Llanelli in the east and within ten miles of Aberystwyth to the north. Several of the smallest rural schools have since closed but there are still over thirty five in existence. There are nine Voluntary Aided schools and the remainder are Voluntary Controlled schools. All the schools are owned by the diocese but they are managed differently. V.A. schools have a closer link to the parish in which they are located. The head teacher must be a communicant member of the Church in Wales and most of the staff are members of that Church. The incumbent of the parish is often Chair of governors of the school and the majority of the governors represent the local parish and are called foundation governors. The governing body has a lot of autonomy and can claim a substantial grant from the State to fund major building programmes. The head teacher of a V.C. school is usually a member of the Church in Wales but there is often less Church presence among the staff. Foundation governors are in the minority but the vicar is almost always a member, sometimes Chair or Vice-Chair. With regard to building projects, repairs etc. only the Local Education Authority decides and funds these. In the Deanery of Cydweli (our deanery) there were two church schools. They were Pentip V.A. School in the town of Llanelli and Ferryside V.C. School eight miles to the west. All church schools must hold a daily Christian Act of Worship and the V.A. schools follow the Church in Wales Syllabus for Religious Education.

The Diocesan Director of Education (or his assistant) has to attend all V.A. school governing body meetings and, when necessary, V.C. school meetings. He has to attend appointment meetings for the posts of head teacher or deputy head teacher and liaise with Local Authority and Welsh Government personnel with regard to school building schemes and administrative matters that directly affect church schools. There is also the wider compass of work in education throughout the diocese like Children's Work, Youth Work and Colleges of Higher and Further Education. Naturally there are officers for all these categories, but the Director has to confer with these officers from time to time. There were also courses for Directors to attend with fellow Education officers of other dioceses and Training Days for governors and staff of schools to be concerned with, even though the Diocesan Schools Officer arranged these. No wonder John Harvey warned me of the onerous task! The worst aspect for me was the travelling. Still I did my best to ensure that the parish did not suffer by my having to balance Director's duties with those of the parish priest. I suppose that, in principle, it appeared that a vicar with only one church was more fortunate than most and could afford to give time to this diocesan work but it should be remembered that the population of the parish of Felinfoel was in excess of six thousand souls. Having only one church does not necessarily mean not being under any pressure in ministry! A rural parish can consist of four churches but have a total population of less than two thousand.

In 1991 the parish began arranging parish holiday "breaks" in which we would take groups of perhaps forty people, not necessarily church members, but friends of members perhaps, to venues such as Chester, the Cheddar and Wells area and Nottingham with its association with lace work and the surrounding Sherwood Forest area and the attractive country houses in Derbyshire. One "holiday" featured Canterbury Cathedral, staying at Maidstone and touring among other places Rye and Hastings. To be fair to the northern province of England we went to York and, apart from the delights of that city and its minster, enjoyed excursions to the Yorkshire Dales and the resort of Whitby. On these "breaks" Sheila would meticulously see to it that as many tastes were catered for as possible and that everyone had choices to explore that suited them. The last venue with Sheila in charge of arrangements was the city of Manchester in 1996 just after an IRA bomb had struck a large hotel quite near to where we were staying. From this base we were able to visit the "set" of the T.V. series, "Coronation Street", explore the Pennines as far as Howarth, famous for its links with the Bronte family, and, naturally, a guided tour of Manchester Cathedral. It was good to "get away" and still enjoy "being together as a parish family".

In 1993 we launched a Parish Visitors group. The aim was to arrange for the group to visit the housebound, those who were ill at home over a long term and the bereaved. Of course the Mothers' Union, who were a very active branch in the parish, had their Indoor

Members' Officer (and a very good one she was too). The branch celebrated the centenary of its founding in 2001 with a service at which the M.U. diocesan chaplain, Canon Bryan Witt, preached and many diocesan officers past and present were in attendance, its link branch in the diocese being Llanstadwel in Pembrokeshire. However this Parish Visitors initiative extended the care and concern of the Church to all church members, irrespective of M.U. membership. It therefore included people of both genders, friends and relatives of church members and generally people who would appreciate a visit. Most of the Visitors went in pairs, some singly. Naturally the vicar visited these people as often as possible and many received Communion from him on a regular basis. The venture was a huge success because it supplemented the vicar's pastoral work. Moreover, at the monthly "update" meetings of the Group, the vicar was able to keep abreast with situations so as to prioritise his own visiting. During the past twenty years much more emphasis has rightly been placed on Lay Ministry, with specific authenticated ministries such as Pastoral Assistants and Eucharistic Assistants. I like to think that our little venture was in a sense a catalyst of things to come. Above all it showed that a show of concern and a friendly chat in the name of the Church was not simply the prerogative of the person wearing a round collar. I am pleased to say that this group continues its splendid work today and I still consider this project to be one of the most satisfying in my entire ministry.

In the same year parishes throughout Wales were required to discuss and decide their opinions on the matter of the proposal to ordain women to the priesthood. Since the Bill was duly passed in 1994 and with so many female clerics having been ordained priest in the meantime, it all seems a long time ago now. In common with other clergy, I spelled out the arguments "for" and "against" the proposal during two successive Sunday morning services when a substantial number of worshippers would be present to listen. Then we convened a meeting open to any who would wish to discuss the matter further. When the whole matter was put to the vote at the meeting of the P.C.C., the Council was evenly divided on the issue. As Chair I gave the casting vote in favour, not simply as a matter of protocol, but out of personal conviction. I am inclined to the view that the percentage of opponents would not have been as high if people had not been persuaded to oppose from a general "conservative" attitude towards gender issues. Views were expressed such as, *"I don't like the idea of a woman at the altar or at the graveside; it does not seem right."* Of course this may be a "knee-jerk" reaction on grounds of biological "hang-ups" about the place of women in society as a whole, in which case it is in complete contradiction with the principle of equality of opportunity in society for all. If, however, we have a *theological* argument for opposing and not a *biological* one, then that is a different matter. What we should guard against is intolerance of one side against the other. There is no place for personal rancour or bitterness. As Christians we can differ in conscience but must respect in charity, as the words of the apostle to the Christians at Ephesus remind us, *"Be completely humble and gentle; be patient, bearing one another in love. Make every effort to keep the unity of spirit in the bond of peace."*

For my sins as an incumbent, I have always been responsible for a churchyard. The churchyard at Felinfoel was a very "popular" one locally. Apart from Dafen churchyard there is only one other Church in Wales burial place in the surrounding area and that is the cemetery in Old Road, in St. Elli's parish. This cemetery was by then "closed" except for the re-opening of family graves. It meant that for many years Holy Trinity churchyard was used to bury those from all parts of the Llanelli area, some of whom had the most tenuous connections with the church at Felinfoel. A plan of sorts had been drawn up in the years after World War 2 but it badly needed updating and there were lots of anomalies in it that had to be addressed. It took several months of my time but eventually a plan was compiled displaying all the graves and the most relevant details on the headstones. From this list the verger and I sifted from the burial registers the known addresses of the deceased persons trusting that, from these facts, and, by conferring with senior church members, we were able to trace the majority of the families concerned. The purpose of this exercise was three-fold (a) to remind the relatives of the deceased of their responsibilities with regard to the upkeep of the grave and (b) to ask each year for a donation towards the grass cutting of the churchyard as a whole which fell to the parish to fund and (c) to inform families from time to time of regulations that apply to churchyard graves laid down by the Church in Wales, as owners of the land. It is surprising how much of a headache it can be to oversee matters such as danger from leaning headstones, rules prohibiting artificial flowers, keeping a grave area free from elaborate efforts to make it a shrine, etc. not to mention the hazards caused by branches needing lopping or storms causing trees to damage graves. Still, from our efforts in compiling a plan with a register of families, we now had secured a means of communication with grave owners especially with regard to acquiring help towards the cost of churchyard maintenance for future years.

Referring to the churchyard reminds me of how communities come together at times of grief with the church as the venue for expressing that common grief. One such tragic occasion I recall vividly was the funeral of nine year old Rebecca (Becky) of the Bear Inn, Felinfoel. Becky was a pupil at Felinfoel Junior School and sadly died of meningitis. The church and the path to the lychgate were thronged with mourners sharing the loss of such a young life from the village. Then there was the tragic accident while on training duty of a young soldier, Martin Rees, aged just seventeen, the son of Peter and Gaynor Rees. Martin was serving with the Royal Artillery in Germany. Again this occasion was marked by a huge congregation and, as this was the period when the situation in Northern Ireland was very volatile, it prompted a huge security operation for us in church. Beside Martin's grave is that of Darrel Roberts, a ship's captain, aged twenty five. He drowned tragically when his ship was travelling off the coast of Southern Ireland. Both of these sad tragedies occurred within a month of each other. "In the midst of life we are in death" – are familiar words from the burial service and they are so true to life. Yet the corollary of this for all who hope for the life eternal is also true, "In the midst of death we are in life."

On a personal note it was just at this time that my own father died in hospital after a short illness.

My brother, Wayne, had been his "prop" during the years after Mam had gone and we had visited as often as possible. His chest condition had never been the same since apparently he had worked in an industrial setting which contained asbestos. The end of an era for the family.

In 1994 I had the double pleasure of recommending two men for acceptance as ordinands. Both were worshipping with us at the time; one had been nurtured in the Faith at Holy Trinity, Mark Soady, and the other nurtured on the hearth of Dafen vicarage, our neighbouring parish, Jonathan Davies. Both trained together at St. Michael's College, Llandaff and were ordained in 1996. Having served their title in the Diocese of St. Davids, Mark and Jonathan are now serving in other dioceses in the Province – Mark as Vicar of Abergavenny and Jonathan as Vicar of Manselton in Swansea. Both priests are a credit to the two parishes that began as two chapels-of-ease to St. Elli's and now find themselves as one united parish of Felinfoel and Dafen. As it happens, both Mark and Jonathan pursued other careers before the call to the ordained ministry became irresistible, as was my own experience.

During the decade of the 1990's our Sunday school slowly diminished in numbers. Like many places we found that Sunday was increasingly becoming a "family out" day to the cost of our attendances. We hit on the idea of a Junior Club which met on Monday after school, the idea being that children of our Sunday school would bring friends and hopefully, through games, Bible quizzes, indoor and outdoor activities, these friends would be attracted to join us on Sunday.

We had a modest success with this idea. Today more and more parishes have recourse to weekdays for children's work, to offset this "Sunday is for recreation only" scenario.

The year 1994 was a memorable one for us as occupants of the vicarage. It was the year when the Diocese decided that the vicarage was no longer a viable residence in terms of its external fabric and its internal maintenance. The roof urgently needed to be renewed, the windows let in water and the grounds were a drain on time and energy. The Diocese determined to build a purpose-built vicarage in the grounds, dispose of the existing house and create two other building plots on the site. In order to accommodate a multi-dwelling site exit, a condition was laid down that the access on to the main road had to be widened. This would necessitate the purchase of a parcel of land from the grounds of the house adjacent to the vicarage drive. Terms were agreed, contracts between purchasers and vendors were drawn up and were about to be signed when, of all things, it was discovered by the Legal Department in Cathedral Road, Cardiff, that a reversion clause was attached to the deeds of the vicarage. This meant that the house could not be disposed of, since, if it became vacant and therefore redundant, it would revert back to the family who originally donated the land. We were now back to Square One. Having built up our hopes of moving into a modern house with considerably less garden to cope with, we were now plunged into a mood of deep despair. Why, oh! Why was this legal obstacle not known about or spotted in the preliminary plans before any decisions were taken about the house's future? As it was, the Parsonage Board had little choice now but to spend on making the house as sound as possible for future years. We were given the choice of living in a rented house or in a caravan on site while the renovations took place. We decided on the caravan simply because we would find it more convenient to pop in and out of the vicarage for cooking facilities or recourse from time to time to items that were stored away there in cupboards. The timing was most unfortunate, however, as the renovations took place from October 1994 until March 1995. Fortunately the roofing contractor had the good fortune to have a dry November for the roof to be completed but the months of December and January were very cold. Still we survived, but only just! In May 1995 we held a grand re-opening of the vicarage with a guided tour of the house available for visitors with stalls, refreshments and a fancy dress competition thrown in for good measure! The vicarage had been given a new lease of life at a cost to the Diocese of £106, 000! However the reality was that the grounds were exactly the same and we were not getting any younger!

In July 1995 an event of a medical kind came to light that turned our lives completely upside down.

Sheila's asthmatic condition was fairly constant by now but of course the stay in the caravan with our having to endure frosty nights and a damp atmosphere were hardly conducive to any asthmatic. She had always suffered from a congenital spondylitis of the spine which resulted in a considerable amount of pain in the top and base of the spine. She had learned to live with these medical ailments over the years. However, for some months she had experienced a different sort of pain in the bottom of the spine, which the G.P. had put down to the usual muscular problems. The problem

was exacerbated during the summer of 1995 by bouts
of vomiting and violent stomach pains. She had scans
and tests which in early September culminated in an
exploratory operation. Shatteringly, we were told that
she had a tumour in the pancreas and that the condition
was inoperable. Typically she made up her mind not to
give in to this chronic situation. Since the condition
of the pancreas is controlled by the intake of food
and the chemical reaction of the enzymes to any
food digested, she adjusted her body to a very strict,
non-toxic, dairy-free diet. She took herself to the Bristol
Medical Centre that treated serious illnesses with a
mixture of homeopathic methods. She was also referred
to the London Homeopathic hospital in London via
St. Luke's hospital for the clergy and their dependents
and even found, through a friend, a faith-healing
practitioner in Ystradgynlais, whose ministrations were
a helpful antidote to the emotional stress. Naturally she
was under the care of an oncologist who was based at
Singleton hospital, Swansea. He arranged sessions of
chemotherapy there and scans from time to time. She
made the supreme effort to attend the Enthronement
Service of Bishop Huw Jones at St. Davids Cathedral in
March 1996. She looked wan and exhausted. It was a
valiant effort on her part to even get there.

Things continued on a fairly even keel until July
1996 when it was discovered that the tumour had
spread and was threatening the lung and the liver.
A new drug from America was tried but to no avail. I
believe that by then the condition was too far advanced.
We celebrated our Silver Wedding Anniversary that year
when many relatives and friends joined us at the
Diplomat Hotel for a lovely gathering. I think everyone

knew from Sheila's appearance that most of them would never see her again. In October that year Sheila celebrated her sixtieth birthday. Close friends of ours, Douglas and Janet Warner, whom we had first met while on holiday in 1972 and with whom we had been in close touch ever since, came from their home in Sussex to stay and to share a birthday meal out with us. It was enjoyable but tinged with an air of inevitability. Just before Christmas anaemia set in and Sheila found that a blood transfusion was required. I recall taking her to the G.P.'s surgery where this was being arranged and her words to the doctor were, *"This is the beginning of the end, isn't it?"* The doctor did not need to hide anything from her about how perilous her condition was. Whatever the medical bulletin, she would want the truth, without any embroidery! We had already made an appointment with the oncologist in the London Homeopathic hospital for January 8th. Despite her extremely weak state she was determined to make the journey to London as long as weather conditions allowed. It had snowed a little a few days before but it was cold and dry when we ventured out. I had to drive us there as there was no way that she could endure the hassle of public transport. I was confident of reaching Euston station which was about a quarter of a mile away from the hospital, but the route thereafter was fraught with one-way systems! I decided to pull into the taxi rank at Euston and hail a taxi which took her there with me following behind. Of course there was nothing that the consultant could tell us that we did not already know. Within three weeks, that is on January 29th. Sheila passed away peacefully and with a dignity that she had always shown in her life.

A good friend of mine, the Revd, Arthur Godsell, officiated at the funeral service. He had been a source of great support to us during Sheila's illness, apart from assisting me with services most willingly since he and Rita had retired to Felinfoel from Essex in 1991. I still miss his bonhomie and amiable personality.

My bereavement of course began in September 1995 not in January 1997. It was the news that she had a terminal condition in a part of the body which is still one of the few areas of medicine in which there has still been little progress in halting the inevitable that struck to the core. For the rest, it was admiration for one whose strength of will was not allowed to diminish and whose spirit could not be quenched. Normally, a patient with such an illness would be fortunate to survive for six to seven months after diagnosis but, in her case, her determination to defy the odds took her to almost eighteen months. I shall never forget that last ever Christmas Carol concert which she directed from her wheelchair and especially her tearful expression at the end when the Trinity Singers acknowledged the applause of the audience, knowing that in that expression was the recognition that this was indeed her farewell performance.

As you can imagine, the next few months were a real trial. Since Sheila's contribution to church worship was such an active one, her absence was felt even more acutely Sunday by Sunday. I took on responsibility for the church choir, being well supported by the faithful adult members. We managed to gain several more children to our ranks. The advantage that the work of a parish priest has over that of many other people is that you try to meet the needs of people when they are at their most vulnerable and, in so doing, you inevitably come across those less fortunate than yourself, which tends to put your own situation in perspective. To some extent this helped. In May 1997 I relinquished my role as Director of Education for the Diocese, after the obligatory five years in the post. The last year or so had been a trial of stamina trying to balance my diocesan and parochial duties against the background of deep anxiety over Sheila's deteriorating condition. My Assistant Director, Canon Derek Evans, ably and most willingly filled the gaps whenever the need arose. The P.C.C. had arranged to hold a Flower Festival that September. Sheila would have been prominent in contributing to its success. Remembering her great interest in flowers it went ahead officially in her memory. Some year or so before, the decision had been taken to refurbish the lychgate, but the plan had to wait for funds to become available(this was the time which saw a sudden large increase in Parish Quota (now called Ministry Share). I resolved that, as Sheila's home church in Sully had a splendid lychgate, it would be appropriate to donate the money needed to complete the work in her memory. The plaque on the lychgate wall today marks the commemoration.

In the summer of 1997 a strange invasion beset the church – a swarm of bees took up residence within its hallowed walls for about two months. Such was its intensity that we had to abandon services in the church one Sunday and hold them in the hall. This unwarranted visit was the more coincidental since we had in the nave a rather splendid stained-glass window depicting Saint Patrick setting off from South Wales by boat to Ireland taking with him the first swarm of bees (allegedly) to make their home in the Emerald Isle. Perhaps the descendants of those pioneer bees had an irresistible urge to revisit the haunts of their long-departed ancestors. After all, "hiraeth" (nostalgia) plays an important part in the make-up of the Welsh.

Preparations for the new Millennium were now progressing. We decided to mark this great milestone by furnishing the church with a new carpet and giving the walls a fresh coat of paint. In the summer of 1999 we held a splendid Summer Fete in the grounds of the vicarage, the weather being gloriously warm. For once the grounds came into their own as an attractive venue for such an occasion. In 1998 I was asked to receive a student in his final year at St. Michael's Theological College on a "placement" in the parish. The main purpose of this step was for him to gain experience of parish life and especially to gain confidence in speaking Welsh. He had begun to learn the language while studying at Aberystwyth University. His name was Ceri Davies, a native of Neath, who had worked in adult education before being accepted for ordination. I enjoyed being his mentor, sharing Morning and Evening Prayer in Welsh each day and taking him around the parish. Ceri also appreciated his midday meals at the vicarage! By now I had become quite adequate in preparing a simple meal while never aspiring to the "cordon bleu" standard! Some years later Ceri returned to the Llanelli area as a member of the Team Ministry of the Benefice of Llanelli.

Shortly after the loss of Sheila I began the challenge of using a computer. I was the most hopeless of novices, and was most grateful to my neighbour, Revd. Bob Hope, a clergyman who had retired from a parish in Weymouth, who patiently answered my frequent cries for help in adversity! The reason for using the computer was not just to improve my professional management of a parish but to help me pursue more effectively a course in Trinity College, Carmarthen, which I started in September 1998. It was a Master's Degree in Church School Studies which had only just emerged as a course that year. I completed the course in the year 2000. At the same time I returned to the role of school inspector. All this was, secretly, a reaction to my bereavement and was my way of dealing with the emotional state in which I now found myself. We all have different responses to a time of stress. Mine was to turn to some academic work as a way of "escape". I think it worked for me at the time. I found it quite enjoyable since I had quite a wide experience of church schools by then. I was not groping in the dark, as it were.

Meanwhile I was coping as best I could with the vicarage garden, admittedly with little zest now as there was no longer the sharing of joy at seeing the first flowers of spring or the enjoyment of the first potatoes from the garden for lunch. Since I had been widowed, Hugh Richards, bless him, came every week to cut that part of the lawn which the sit-on mower could not tackle. This was a great help to me.

In 1999 I was invited by the head teacher of Pentip School to take a R.E. lesson each week with Year 6 pupils. It was good to make direct contact again with school life at ground level. At more or less the same time I was unexpectedly given an opportunity to represent the clergy of the deanery as a member of the governing body of St. John Lloyd R.C. High School in

Llanelli. This was one of only two V.A. schools at secondary level in the diocese of St. Davids. Moreover, these schools, though owned by the Roman Catholic Church, were committed to accepting a high proportion of pupils from other Christian traditions, notably the Church in Wales. As the C. in W. had no similar high school in the diocese, to be a member of this governing body gave me an insight into the provision of Christian Education at the next stage from the primary school. For example, many Pentip School pupils furthered their Christian education by going on to St. John Lloyd School.

Things were starting to fall into place again. I was resuming my interest in education without being tied to the stress of responsibility that I once had when involved as an officer at diocesan level.

It was during one of my weekly lessons at Pentip School early in 1999 that I happened to ask the class if they had any interest in joining a church choir, assuming that they were not already committed to another church in this way and invited them to try it out. Two pupils responded positively. One was Warren Thomas who came and seemed to enjoy his place in the choir. I duly met Mrs Gwendoline Thomas when she came to collect Warren from practice each Wednesday. They had both been regular worshippers at All Saints, Llanelli. Now both became members of Holy Trinity, since it was pointless her dropping the boy off and then worship elsewhere as a communicant herself. We thus gained a chorister and a member of the congregation. I began to see Gwendoline socially. She was easy to relate to and to confide in. During the coming months our friendship deepened. In August 2000 the National Eisteddfod came to Llanelli and I had arranged for two people from North Wales to stay in the vicarage who were acting as stewards at the Eisteddfod pavilion. Doug and Janet came to stay for the week to assist with hospitality and with the ability of Gwendoline to converse a little in Welsh, the guests were made to feel at home. Unfortunately, I developed a tummy virus at the start of that week and, to my dismay, was admitted to hospital for three days for monitoring. So, by the time I had gained my strength again, the Eisteddfod passed me by! However I do not know how I could have managed without my "locum hosts!" It all helped me to see that Gwendoline was someone I could rely on in a practical way "as a partner in time of difficulty" and with whom I felt entirely at ease, apart from her showing herself to be very solicitous for my welfare.

That summer we announced our engagement. She had been widowed in her 40's and had a grown up son and daughter, the son having just had their first child. We both needed and appreciated a relationship in which we were companionable and fulfilled. The wedding was to be held at Holy Trinity on February 24th. (St. Matthias's Day) in 2001. My good and much lamented friend, the Revd. Noel Gillman, was kind enough to accept my invitation to solemnise the ceremony.

With my second marriage in the offing, I reflected during the months that followed our engagement whether it would be a good thing to remain in the parish with all its memories. I recall having recently composed the millennium hymn (See the Appendix) reflecting on how Bishop Huw had asked my consent for it to be sung at the Diocesan Missionary Festival. This was the only time, by the way, that a bishop has asked *me* permission to do anything in my entire life! During my conversation with the bishop I shared with him my thoughts about a new relationship requiring a new start in pastures new. I have to admit that when I arrived at Felinfoel I had assumed that I would be in residence for the rest of my ministry. But one has to adjust to new situations. This is what ministry and indeed the whole of life is all about. The parish of Penbre with Llandyry happened to become vacant in September, 2000. It was not far from established family and friends, it had just two churches and was not too heavily populated. The appointment of a new incumbent was in the gift of the bishop himself. Knowing my personal feelings about uprooting myself because of the new situation, Bishop Huw concurred entirely with my sentiments and promptly offered me the parish.

When in October 2000 my decision was announced in church, Hugh Richards commented afterwards, "*So you are breaking the mould, vicar. Every incumbent has by tradition, retired from this parish, not resigned and moved on.*" "*Who said I was a traditionalist?*" I replied, "*At 59, I have a new wife and a new family to relate to!*"

I remembered Sheila's words during the last weeks of her illness, "*I hope you will find someone else in life; you deserve it.*" I had spent twelve eventful and satisfying years in Felinfoel. It had been a period of ebb and flow in fortune. Little did I realise then that I would be in fact the last incumbent of a parish that had existed since 1887. A new millennium had begun and I was preparing to make my final move before hanging up my boots! A tranquil few years to end my ministerial career? If I have learned one thing in life, it is this, "Expect only the unexpected!"

CHAPTER 9

THE SHIP'S LAST VOYAGE

At the age of 59, one would hardly be contemplating a spate of church renovation and restoration but I had a premonition of what lay ahead of me. After my appointment to Pembrey with Llandyry was known,

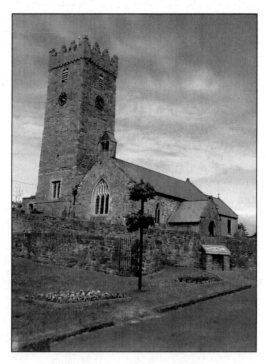

St. Illtyd's church, Pembrey

I was invited to join the Archdeacon of Carmarthen, the Venerable Anthony Crockett, later to be Bishop of Bangor (and a product of Pontypridd boys' grammar school himself), to a meeting with the churchwardens and Cadw's Senior Building Consultant at St. Illtyd's Church, Pembrey to discuss the proposed plans for restoring the parish church. Cadw of course is the body that cares for buildings of architectural and historical interest in Wales. I was there strictly as an observer and listener but the meeting gave me a useful insight into the background of the structure and the reason for Cadw's presence at this site meeting. I was to know a lot more after my installation took place.

We moved into the vicarage at Pembrey in March 2001. Pembrey lies five miles west of Llanelli on the road to Carmarthen. The house has been described as commanding the most enviable views in the diocese. It stands in an elevated position looking across to the Worms Head at the western tip of the Gower, while immediately below are the Ashburnham Golf Course and the Pembrey Country Park. The vicarage looks down therefore with gleaming eye on golfers and leisure seekers! The house dates from the early 1930's when the more discerning Diocesan Parsonage Boards were beginning to dispose of the old, rambling Victorian buildings in favour of less pretentious but more practical homes for clergy to occupy. It was without doubt (apart from the modern house in the Rhondda), the most comfortable and manageable vicarage in which I had resided. On our first tour of inspection of the house the Archdeacon suggested that an area under the kitchen top would be ideal for a dishwasher. Gwendoline's prompt reply, looking in my direction, was, "*Oh!*

I already have a mobile dishwasher with two hands and two feet!" We still have no dishwasher (by mutual agreement) and so my hands are still fully employed at the kitchen sink! The garden, once some heavy digging was done to clear one area of rough appearance to create a small vegetable plot, was a "walkover" for someone who had been so used to "mega" grounds. The only challenge of any consequence was to keep the tall hedge facing the road under control – this would be no insurmountable problem for someone of my enforced horticultural experience.

Having seen the "parish profile" which highlights the priorities that the parish look for in their new incumbent, I was gratified to see potential for sound relationships between priest and people. The qualities that the parish was looking for were: (1) a priest who is approachable (2) a male or female priest equally welcomed (3) a priest committed to caring for the flock and building up good relationships. It appeared to me that in this fertile soil seeds of a progressive and collaborative ministry could be sown. I shall always remember an Institution sermon in which a bishop declared that in a year from then he would want to know, not how the new vicar was getting on, but *"how you, the people, are progressing under his guidance."* The arrival of a new incumbent is a challenge for clergy *and* people to respond to in a spirit of togetherness in ministry.

Within a few months of settling in we were embroiled in preparing details for the Building Project of St. Illtyd's church. It involved a complete re-roofing and the re-plastering of the interior walls. The plastering had only been removed some 15 years before to be replaced by a dressed stone finish, which, despite its commendable craftsmanship had, aesthetically, a somewhat overpowering effect, perhaps, on what was a modest-sized building. Cadw's concern was that their advice had not been sought about such a change to the church's appearance and that the walls had to revert to the plaster that was always a feature of a medieval church with a coating of lime wash for resistance to dampness. Since the church was a Listed A category building with regard to architectural and historical interest, Cadw were pledged to funding the project almost entirely but, against that, the parish were obliged to follow the guidelines that they laid down in respect of implementing the restoration work. The roof would form Stage 1 of the project and the re-plastering of the walls would form Stage 2. The whole project was to take almost two years to complete. I had my initiation into confirming architect's drawings, monitoring costing and the consideration of contingency plans. We were fortunate in having professional people among our church membership to oversee these matters – Hywel Davies, the Project Manager, was a recently retired Chief Executive of Highways for Carmarthenshire and Bryan Bevan, our church treasurer, who was a professional accountant, both of whom kept us on course to achieve our aim. With these capable people at our disposal, the role left for me to fulfil was mainly the sending of letters to explain our eligibility for this and that to be done as the need arose and, generally, to support and oversee the progress of work. I recall going up to inspect the roof as the workmen were putting the finishing touches to its renewal. There was a hubbub of talking as I ascended the ladder. Then I heard a hoarse cry, *"Watch your language, boys, the padre's on his way!"* As I got to the top, a sudden and unnatural silence descended. It's strange the difference a clergyman can make to a situation without any action on his part! Once the roof was completed, I could sit in my vicar's stall, confident that no drops of water would splash on my head, as I had been in the direct firing line of a trickle of rainwater ever since I had begun to take services in the church. But then, when is the vicar *not* in the firing line?

With Stage 2 pending it was time to vacate the church temporarily for the walls to be dealt with. We were fortunate in obtaining the facilities of Hermon Wesleyan church in Pembrey for a period of eight months. The Sunday services there being in the afternoon, the church was at our disposal for mornings and evenings. Despite not being familiar with the design of the building, we made the best of the situation. Indeed the compact size of the church forced the congregation to sit closer together and, with the vicar located in no far off chancel or sanctuary, it made for a very warm sense of belonging. We finally returned to head-quarters for the Harvest Festival services of 2003. I fancy that the familiar Harvest hymns, *"Come, ye thankful people, come"* and *"To thee our grateful hymn of praise"* struck an even heartier note that year! However, we were extremely grateful to Hermon for their kind gesture to us. From the very outset, then, I was thrust into a "baptism of fire" in this my final parish. Still they say that a church in which plenty of activity goes on engenders a greater sense of purpose!

St.Illtyd's church is right in the centre of the village. The name "Pembrey" is an anglicised form of the Welsh "Penbre" which means "end of the hill"- an appropriate description of a village located where "Pembrey Mountain ends" and the village itself begins. The village lies sandwiched betwixt hill and sea. I always feel that the village square is reminiscent of many a typical English village scene than the more shapeless Welsh village, with its two public houses and, until a few decades ago, its couple of shops and its post office (still open!). Lording it over the inhabitants on a rise of ground was the church. Across the road from the church was the Old Vicarage, which was the original vicarage until 1931 when the less onerous house was built about 200 yards up Mountain Road. Despite recent small housing developments, Pembrey retained the distinctive atmosphere of a village. The church itself had a long history and possessed a charm and homeliness about it that marked it out as medieval. It was the "mother church" of a vast geographical area until 1951, extending to the western edge of Llanelli on the east, to the border with Cydweli parish on the west and to beyond Trimsaran on the north. The great centre of population within it was the town of Burry Port. The parish was served by four churches, Pembrey, Llandyry (serving Trimsaran), Burry Port and Pwll. In 1951 the parish was divided between Pembrey and Llandyry to the west and Burry Port and Pwll to the east, each with its incumbent. The parish once boasted a staff of a vicar and three curates, one curate based in Llandyry, one in Burry Port and another in Pwll. Two of those curates later became respectively a dean and a bishop in the diocese. I refer to Dean Lawrence Bowen (a native of Felinfoel, incidentally) and Bishop John Richards (who later became the vicar of my own parish of Pontypridd,) I would never have imagined that one day I would be the incumbent of a parish where the vicar I knew as a young teenager had learned his "trade" as a priest. Here again is an example of having seen people a second time round in a different light.

The church of St. Illtyd was almost certainly an original Celtic foundation, though most of the present building dates from the 13th to 15th century. The original font, said to date from the 13th century, was now located, for observation only, in the Lady Chapel. The lofty tower was the oldest part of the structure with its three clocks, no clock being installed on its eastern side, that is, the side facing Burry Port. Local tradition has it that when Burry Port spread its wings to become the more urban community it is today, there arose a resentment among the more traditional, rural inhabitants of Pembrey. This antipathy found expression in deciding that the people of Burry Port did not deserve to benefit from a glance at a clock in the tower of their church. Mind you, it could be that the good people of Burry Port were such good time keepers that they did not need to look at a clock! There were three bells in the tower dating for 1552. This was the third church in which I had served that had its own belfry; St. Catherine's, Pontypridd had a fine peal and St. Peter's in the Rhondda had a splendid peal. There is something very meaningful about bells summoning people to church or conveying a message of sadness at a funeral or joy at a wedding that stirs the heart. I love to hear bells pealing the notes of a hymn tune, thus setting the scene for worship.

The church also boasted an Elizabethan chalice and the admirer of medieval architecture would have appreciated the sixteenth century timber barrel roof and the "squint" in the wall on the south side of the chancel, to allow the congregation a "peep" at what was happening at the altar in the Mass in pre-Reformation days. I loved the seventeenth century Communion rail whose almost semi-circular design gave the impression of a "family around the table," as they received the sacrament. The outer door of the church bears a unique inscription in Latin, dating from 1717 which says: *This is the house of God and this is the gate of Heaven"*. Visitors from afar came to see the famous stone plaque in the exterior south wall. This commemorated a tragedy at sea in which a niece of Emperor Napoleon Bonaparte, Josephine, drowned when the ship in which she was travelling went aground on Cefn Sidan sands. The body itself was removed to France for burial. The church burial ground at St. Illtyd's was a large one of uneven ground levels. It contained a number of war graves of service personnel who died in World War 2, many of whom were Polish. A short memorial service for the large Polish contingent now living in the Llanelli area was held each year in the churchyard on All Saints' Day (the traditional Polish Day of Remembrance for war victims.)

Referring to the churchyard and its maintenance I must single out the responsible way in which our People's Warden, Brynmor Morgan, oversaw the problems that beset every parish with a churchyard. His personal diligence and care went beyond the remit of what a churchwarden is required to show, being on hand to help with any task without being asked.

One major event focusing on a particular grave in the churchyard was the special visit to the church in June 2003 of members of the Dalton Genealogical

Society. This society had members drawn from all over the globe. They came to Pembrey that year for their annual reunion, about sixty of them, some from as far as South America and Canada, to join us for worship. After morning service prayers of commemoration were said at the grave of James Dalton who died in 1721, the son of Walter Dalton, a native of Whitney, who is buried in the chancel of the church. Another member of the family, Charles, was a former churchwarden of Pembrey. His name appears on the outer door under the Latin inscription, mentioned above.

It was easy to see why Cadw and all those who care for the upkeep of our churches rated this church a building of quality and of historical interest that needed careful and appropriate preservation. This was why we were so fortunate in having Hywel as our Project Manager who could speak the language of building inspectors, architects and the like on our behalf. With my allegedly gift for putting any of our concerns in writing as the need arose (a task all clergy have thrust on them most of the time) the whole project was a good example of how clergy and able lay people can work together at a crucial time and produce a satisfying result.

The size of the church hall was ideal for the routine activities like Sunday school, church group meetings, coffee mornings and the like, but for the bigger events such as the Mothers' Union Christmas Fair we had to use the Memorial Hall just up the road. The Mothers' Union was a strong organisation that was served by successive faithful officers. It supported all the deanery and diocesan events with enthusiasm, their link branch being Steynton in Pembrokeshire. Two popular and successful coffee mornings held every year in the church hall were on Shrove Tuesday and one held in aid of the Macmillan Nurses in September. Unfortunately Llandyry had no church hall but a group of ladies were members of the parish M.U. branch and a number of worshippers faithfully supported the larger social events held in Pembrey.

I was only a few months into my ministry in the parish when I received a shock to the system that had nothing whatsoever to do with church routine. Warren had two of his school pals from St. John Lloyd School to spend the day with him. He asked me to show them the tower of the church, see the splendid view from the top and observe the way the bells worked. As we returned to the house, Warren answered a message on his mobile phone, seemingly to confirm to the person concerned that we were a few yards from arriving home. As we turned in through the gate, we saw the forecourt jammed with cars! I thought, "Whatever is going on here? Have I been found out at last to be a heretic and these people have come to gloat over my discomfort?" As I entered the lounge I was faced with a room thronged with people singing, "Happy birthday to you!" Gwendoline had secretly arranged for people from our new parish and friends from Felinfoel to join together to celebrate my sixtieth birthday. Having recovered from the shock, I was delighted to meet everyone so unexpectedly. The request to go to the church tower was just a ploy to get me out of the way while guests arrived, of course. This was not to be the only time that Gwendoline would spring a surprise twist to an event!

The daughter church of the parish was Llandyry, the chapel-of-ease to St. Illtyd's. It stands about three and a half miles north-west of Pembrey in the scattered rural setting of Pinged and about half a mile from the former mining village of Trimsaran. The Welsh name Llandyry has been the subject of much speculation. Some have taken it to be a variation of Llanderw, meaning "church among the oak trees" while others maintain that it refers to the fact that an original wooden building stood on the site because they take the name to mean "church made of oak". It originated as a stopping off point of prayer for pilgrims on their way from Pembrey to Cydweli, such pilgrims having to make a long detour then to cross the Gwendraeth River at Spudder's Bridge which straddles the border between the two parishes. Today Llandyry serves the communities of Pinged and Trimsaran.

The cruciform building, holding about 130 people, consisted of chancel, nave, transepts, entrance porch and vestry. Its inclusion in land deeds of the time points to its having been founded in the early part of the 16th century. The church was completely restored in 1826 and in 1904 it was extended at its west end with a small bell-cote added. The registers dated from 1904, previous entries having been recorded in Pembrey church. A strange feature of the church was that the chancel had been so designed that it inclined to the north so that the chancel and nave were not in line. This was alleged to be a symbol of the head of Christ inclining on the cross of crucifixion.

There was a certain tranquil aura about the setting of Llandyry that I sensed as soon as I became familiar with it. This was particularly noticeable when officiating at a burial service in the churchyard. It was as though the words at the committal of the body to be buried,

"I heard a voice saying to me, "Blessed are the dead who die in the Lord from henceforth. "Even so," says the spirit "that they may rest from their labours," had indeed been truly fulfilled in the restful scene as we stood at the graveside to commend the soul of the departed to God's eternal rest.

Opposite the church stood the imposing Llandyry House. There is some evidence that points to the possibility that this was the original site of the church and that later it was rebuilt on the other side of the road. The house had been built in the 19th century to provide accommodation for one of the curates of the parish. A series of curates resided there until the 1950's. With the former parish of Pembrey being down-sized to its present state, the house was sold. However there was a curate residing in Trimsaran until 1976. One of my first duties in Llandyry was to order a headstone for the grave of a former curate who died while residing at Llandyry House but whose headstone had never been erected. He was the Revd. Daniel Harries who died in 1930, aged just forty two.

Until 1983 when the last coal train travelled to Burry Port there was a railway system linking the Gwendraeth mining communities through Pembrey to the harbour at Burry Port, where the coal was exported to Devon, Cornwall or beyond. What a tourist attraction a passenger train would have been today and a considerable saving of time of journey for travellers by car from say Pontyberem to Burry Port. The last passenger train to use the track was in 1953.

The Sunday services in both churches were in English and Welsh alternately. On any 5th Sunday (once a quarter) we held a bilingual Eucharist in Pembrey and on the 4th Sunday a bilingual service of Morning Prayer at Llandyry. A minibus brought worshippers to Llandyry from Trimsaran each Sunday. This was undoubtedly the strongest Welsh-speaking parish of my whole ministry. Many funerals were conducted partly or even entirely in Welsh. Thus in order to relate fully to the community, it was essential for the vicar to be reasonably fluent in that language. Gwendoline held a weekly conversational class for children from Pembrey school for about a year, she having lost the Welsh she had spoken in early childhood. She found it made her more confident in speaking Welsh herself when guiding children's conversational skills.

A feature of this parish which marked it out as a semi-rural community was the way in which the vicar was invited and indeed expected in many cases to attend events that had nothing directly to do with church affairs; the annual Gardening and Crafts Show at Pembrey, the special anniversary of the founding of the Senior Citizens Group in Trimsaran etc.. Congregations were not as numerous as my previous parishes but they were perhaps more consistent. One felt also that there was a more respectful regard for the place of the Church in the community at large. A sociologist may well attribute this to a pattern of life that was more stable, probably less secularised, the further west one travelled.

We had a fairly strong Sunday school at Pembrey with a Family Service every other month for parents and children. An increasing number of parents began to show an interest in taking a class, which increased the chances of maintaining our numbers and encouraged family attendance at church. I found that as many adults came forward for confirmation as young people. The net result was usually more commitment to church-going as communicants afterwards. There were excellent links with the two primary schools at Pembrey and Trimsaran. Pembrey School held a Christmas Nativity Play and a moving Passiontide Drama telling the story of Christ's last week on earth each year in church. Also there were many educational visits to the church and the churchyard as part of pupils' projects in the history of their local area. Trimsaran School attended Llandyry church for Harvest Festival and the parents and children of the Bobl Bach Family Centre attended the Christingle services there. I found myself directly involved in an Estyn inspection of each school, leading an assembly. It was quite a change for me to be on the receiving end of the inspectors' attention! As a regular visitor to both schools, the head teachers of both schools assumed that I deserved this doubtful honour!

A popular highlight of the year was the Summer Garden Party held in the grounds of Bryn Illtyd Home, Pembrey. Here again we have an example of the Church in close contact with the local community. Mr and Mrs James were not only gracious enough to offer the facilities of their Home but personally contributed to giving help on the day. Even though it involved much work there was a relaxed, happy atmosphere which I always find an outdoor event at a pleasant venue has. On two occasions I allowed myself to be the victim of the historical "punishment in the stocks" being subjected to assaults from soapy sponges. Was it my imagination but were some assaults so robust that the perpetrators were only too pleased to get their own back on one who bored them with his over-long sermons? The Garden Party was always blessed with good weather and financially very successful. One year however our faith was sorely tried when it rained until about 11 a.m. on the day but mercifully cleared up in time to give us a gloriously sunny afternoon ("the devil looks after his own!")

Gwendoline organised a parish holiday to Chester which was thoroughly enjoyed by about 40 people. Besides visiting the splendid cathedral, formerly Benedictine Abbey church of St. Werburgh, we explored the exquisite shopping galleries and cobbled alleyways but did not have time unfortunately to attend horse racing at the oldest racecourse in the country! The Queen's Hotel near the railway station did us proud with regard to comfort and food. One amusing incident was when my cousin Mary, aged eighty at the time, was invited to try sitting on such a "high throne" in the hotel foyer that her feet were left dangling two feet above the floor, Gwendoline and I both called out in banter, *"Ma'm, now who's Mary, the Queen Mother?"* This was an appropriate remark since cousin Mary was a great fan of the Royal Family herself. Gwendoline also arranged a pre-Christmas excursion to the exqui-site village in the Yorkshire Dales of Grassington, to sample the festive atmosphere of the Christmas market, a Nativity play through the cobbled street and the lovely Dales scenery. About sixteen people went, mainly from the Llandyry congregation. Naturally, with Gwendoline's attention to detail, everything was arranged with efficiency. She was so confident in handling money and getting the "best offers" available, something I, for one, am content to leave to others.

Enjoyable day trips were arranged to the Cardiff Ice Show for several years, an event that delighted spectators aged from five to seventy five (or even higher!)

It may be that cynics are urged to ask "What do all such events have to do with proclaiming the Gospel and making disciples of people?" For answer I turn to Scripture and observe there how Jesus truly *shared his ministry* with his team of disciples. Yes! – Jesus taught them, Yes! – he healed the needy, but he took time also to eat with them and admire the lilies of the field and delight in journeys they shared to the well of Jacob, to the mount of Transfiguration, not to mention the market-place. There are so many ways in which the truth of the Gospel can be conveyed to us. It is too great to be limited to boundaries of our own making.

One of the duties placed on me when I arrived in the parish was to direct St. Illtyd's church choir, since there was nobody else willing, apparently, to fill the role. I reluctantly accepted as the choir included adults with experience of singing well and deserved support, yet mindful of the commitment involved when faced also with parochial duties. The choosing of suitable music for the voices available is always the most onerous task, especially with simple anthems at Festivals. Having said this, it was good to have the help of three altos, quite a luxury for many parish choirs. We also had three accomplished accompanists to call on, one of whom was a soloist of local renown in her own right, Elizabeth Bevan. Thus we were extremely well blessed, especially when nowadays organists and singers who are willing to give the commitment to Sunday by Sunday worship are such a rare breed! The first year into the parish and the choir went to sing carols at the home of three elderly sisters who had links with Pembrey church. They lived in Silver Terrace in Burry Port. Two of them were in their nineties and the youngest well in her eighties. They were absolutely thrilled that we had taken the trouble to come on a cold night to sing to them. I was not sure which was the warmer of the two - the roaring open coal fire in the living room of their terraced house where we twelve choristers were gathered with our hostesses, or the warmth of the welcome and appreciation on the faces of the three residents! Sadly, within three months the eldest, bed-ridden sister had died and six months later still, another passed away. The youngest spent her last few years in a local nursing home. I was gratified that the choir had given what proved to be their last Christmas together in Silver Terrace something to warm their hearts. Is not this what the spirit of Christmas is all about?

One of the very successful aspects of parish activity was the fortnightly Bible Study Group. We averaged about twelve to fifteen in number. One of our contingent came as often as possible from Bryn Illtyd Home and he was ninety three! Gilbert Davies, a former teacher, was a splendid, perceptive contributor to our discussions. We also benefited from the able company of the Revd. John Ablett, a retired priest, who was a native of Essex. John was always willing to cover for me when I was on holiday or in residence at the cathedral with regard to Sunday services and funerals but also willing to take the Bible Study Group when I was unavailable on occasions. This group was not only a means of exploring our faith but of deepening our fellowship as we shared our deepest thoughts and ideas together. In the pulpit the vicar is perceived to be the proverbial "six feet above criticism", whereas in a study or prayer circle he is there to listen as much as to speak. In Felinfoel we had followed the Emmaus Course that was produced in the mid 1990's to promote a deepening of the faith of those who had been nurtured in belief, unlike the Alpha course which is intended primarily for the "unchurched". The same experience of fellowship marked that parish group also. Such groups, sometimes called "house groups" when held in homes of the parish, are usually and perhaps inevitably small in numbers attending but they are known for the enthusiasm and commitment to the group that they encourage. We ought not to measure success always in terms of numbers but by the blessing and spiritual insight received. This was certainly true of our experience in Llandyry also when we met to discuss the course "Venturing in Mission". For a church without the facility of a hall this was an opportunity for sharing informally what group members believed in a way that helped each one to know themselves better as Christians. One member of the group, Susie Rogers, came every week from Bryncethin, near Bridgend, so there must have been a solid motivation! She had come to worship quite regularly at Llandyry through her marriage to someone who had been nurtured there as a boy.

In villages like Pembrey and Trimsaran there tend to be warm relationships between Christian churches. Special occasions in the Christian Year such as Harvest were supported as a community of Christians, for example. In addition we arranged Advent Carol services together and Christian Aid projects were organised ecumenically. Fellow clergy participated in funeral services at our churches when the deceased or the bereaved family were known to them. I had the good fortune to be able to relate to those ministers responsible for their churches in the parish even if they themselves did not reside in the area so that co-operation was possible in this important extension of the Family of God. I am pleased to say that this good relationship between churches continues today in the parish.

Parishes throw up certain characters that are apt to stay in one's mind. Two such people present themselves to me now – one passed away soon after reaching her 100th birthday and the other is still going strong as this book goes to print at the ripe age of 102! Gwyneth Jones was the oldest member of Llandyry who still attended church during my time as incumbent. She was the widow of a former parish priest, Revd. John Jones, former vicar of Llangyndeyrn. John and Gwyneth achieved the feat of walking the China Wall together *after* John retired. She was an active M.U. member throughout her life and Chair of Trimsaran Senior Citizens Group for many years. Gwyneth had a sharp mind. She often knew more about what went on in the diocese than I did and was never afraid to speak her mind about what went on! Though her sight deteriorated in later years her capacity for listening intently never waned. Hardly a service passed by without her making a comment about what was said in the sermon – either by way of a pertinent question or else a useful addition to what had been said from her own experience of life! These "exchanges" were useful to me as ammunition for material in later sermons.

Bessie Williams still attends church as a centenarian. Surely there cannot be many such people around! she had been licensee of the "Ship Aground", a public house in Ashburnham Road, Pembrey. She liked to look the elegant hostess at home or when out and about, even if she no longer served her former "customers". She had retained a lively interest in what went on in village and church and still attended the Sunday evening services when she could. One of the greatest thrills I have had, pastorally, was to see her at our service of Lessons and Carols on New Year's Eve (as it happened that year), which coincided with her birthday. Before singing our last carol I invited the congregation to join in singing "Happy Birthday" to Bessie, celebrating ninety three years young! What a shining example of those, in the words of the prophet Isaiah, *"who will run and not grow weary, they will walk and not faint."*

Within a year of completing the Building Programme at St. Illtyd's we had to turn our attention to the needs of Llandyry as a building. It had been obvious to me when I first visited the church after accepting the nomination to the parish and viewed the patches of mould on the walls that an underlying problem needed to be put right. There had been no plans to restore the church before I arrived, as at St. Illtyd's, but a Quinquennial (5 yearly) Inspection in 2003 confirmed that restoration work was urgently needed. The church was listed B Category by Cadw as of modest architectural and historical interest, so we had to confer with them before any firm preparations could be made. We had to be guided by their recommendations even though we had to bear the cost ourselves! In the spring of 2004 we set up a Llandyry Restoration Fund. Our Project Manager was Vincent Lloyd, who, apart from being a churchwarden of many years standing was also church treasurer and secretary of the Diocesan Board of

Finance, and therefore a most able administrator. Naturally the Project was in the safest of hands! How fortunate we were as a parish to have such able people.

We set up a Restoration Fund and letters of Appeal were sent to as many households in the area as possible, explaining the part Llandyry had played in the history of the local community. This brought in an income of over £20,000 which showed the measure of affection in which the church was held by local inhabitants. We organised a sponsored walk from Llandyry church to St. Illtyd's, one participant being my cousin Mary who covered the distance in her motor scooter. So she was technically doing a "sponsored wheelie." No matter! Then came the news we were eagerly waiting for. The Heritage Lottery Fund was pleased to award us a grant of £60,000. There is no doubt that without this boost of good fortune, we could not have afforded to restore the church in its entirety. We still had a "mountain to climb" financially, so we set about arranging fund-raising meals at a local Indian restaurant which had a policy of returning 50% of the cost of a meal to the customer to any charitable organisation. These pleasant occasions (with little work attached to them on the part of church members) were well supported by parishioners of both churches with Gwendoline doing sterling work in co-ordinating efforts to ensure that tickets were circulated.

The work at the church could now commence and indeed lasted from February 2006 until September of that year. During that period we were fortunate in having the facilities of Noddfa Independent chapel for Sunday services since the church was "out of bounds". On Easter Day and Whit Sunday that year Llandyry worshippers joined those at Pembrey. Finally, as a last-ditch effort to make up the shortfall we organised a super sponsored walk of fourteen miles from Bryn outside Llanelli down to the Millennium Coastal Path at Morfa and along it, to end up in Pembrey Church Hall. Only fifteen participated but they were so handsomely sponsored by well-wishers and, with Barclays Bank promoting our efforts to double the total money collected, we were able to amass a grand total of £14,000. The first person to complete the walk was seventy eight year old Cecil Street. Here was another who heeded the words of the prophet Isaiah when he said, *"Those who wait on the Lord shall renew their strength"*. Although the walk was held early in November we were rewarded by warm, bright weather. Obviously the sun shone on the righteous that day! (The devil had the day off!). Completion of the work had coincided with the Harvest Festival when the then Dean of St. Davids, the Very Revd. J. Wyn Evans, was our preacher. (The dean's mother once taught in Trimsaran so that coming to Llandyry brought back childhood memories for him). The Restoration received Bishop Carl Cooper's blessing and re-dedication a few weeks later. After the service, attended by former clergy of the parish and led by the choir of St. Illtyd's, we had recourse to the Welfare Hall in Trimsaran where the choir sang a parody of the Harvest hymn; along the lines of,

> *"Come, you grateful people, come,*
> *Now the church her prize has won,*
> *Walls resplendent, shining paint,*
> *Gladdening hearts of every saint"* etc.

We had succeeded in doing what we could to promote the glory of God's House for years to come.

Considering the small but faithful band of worshippers that attended Llandyry, it was a splendid all-round effort, supported in no small way by members of the parish church too.

Some very poignant funeral services of young people marked my period in office. Again, they were examples of the community coming together to mourn as one at times when the loss is felt by all. In my first year as vicar, Pembrey saw the tragic death by accident of soldier Robert Hall of Burry Port in his twenties. Then came the passing of David Rowlands; David had a rare heart condition and he collapsed and died at home. There was also a moving memorial service to him in Sir Gâr College, Llanelli where he had been a popular student. Philip Francis, whose younger sister Lindy was a member of our church choir, had a fatal accident on the nearby railway track. Philip was only nineteen. Christian Ford, a popular rugby player, collapsed and died of natural causes while playing at a local game. On New Year's Eve, Matthew Kelly was killed in a car accident in Trimsaran. He was only fifteen and his friend, Alexei, aged nineteen, the driver of the car, was also killed.

These moving occasions and so many more, point to the way in which we clergy minister to families in all kinds of circumstances, standing alongside them in their grief, as the whole community did on these sad occasions.

I should mention two funerals of faithful church members during my period as vicar, one at Pembrey and the other at Llandyry, that drew large congregations, and deservedly so. One was the funeral of John Nicholson of Pembrey. John was a notable historian of the locality, having written books on the history of the church and aspects of the community. He was a lifelong member of the Carmarthenshire Antiquarian Society. If you wanted to know anything about Pembrey's past, he was your man! Above all, it was a joy to be in the company of someone who was a true gentleman. One of the saddest losses among the faithful at Llandyry in my time was the passing of the People's Warden, William Gravell of Trimsaran. William was a true man of the people whose loyalty to his church and closeness to the people he represented were second to none – of a cheerful, amiable personality, he was an example to any would-be People's Warden and a great loss to the congregation.

In 2003 Bishop Carl Cooper set up a panel of three Advisers on Vocations to Ministry in the diocese, one for each archdeaconry, and asked me to be Adviser for the Archdeaconry of Carmarthen. Our remit was to meet informally with those who wished to explore and test their calling not only to the sacred ministry but to various lay ministries as Readers, Worship Leaders, Pastoral Assistants etc. One of those that sought my help was the Revd. Richard Wood who was later ordained and became the curate of Aberaeron and then Team Vicar in the Benefice of Llanelli. It was very satisfying helping these people to evaluate what their calling meant to them and how the Church could meet their needs. It took me back to the old days of teaching six formers in school, (not that any age barrier came into this equation). From time to time we brought people together of similar aspirations for a brainstorming session and fellowship, to share ideas and learn from one another's experiences.

I mentioned earlier in this chapter that my duties in the parish were being covered while I was "in residence". This refers to my appointment in 1994 as Canon in Residence at the cathedral. So much of note happened that year in the parish of Felinfoel that I felt it wiser to say something about my time as Residential Canon here. At least I was following the tradition of incumbents of Felinfoel in this regard; - they all became canons while resident in that parish.

How do you become a canon? What does a canon do? Good questions! A canon is appointed by the bishop, usually for services rendered over and above his or her parochial duties. Mine came about presumably for my involvement in Church Education. Most Diocesan Directors of Education are made canons in virtue of this role. A canon is a member of the cathedral chapter helping the Dean to manage the affairs of the cathedral. The residential canon has a stall assigned to him in the cathedral in which he sits during any service that takes place in the chancel. He preaches at one of the Sung Services on the Sundays that he is in residence and the Welsh-speaking canon also officiates at the Welsh service on Sundays, which is held in the Lady Chapel. He attends and takes part in the daily morning and evening services held in the chancel. He is also expected to spend part of his day making himself available to welcome visitors and, if necessary, show them around the cathedral. If the dean is absent from the Sunday service, it is the canon who gives the blessing at the end, as he is next in seniority to the dean at any cathedral service. Honorary canons do not reside in the canonry but are invited to preach at the cathedral, usually twice a year. What was an unforgettable privilege for me as canon in residence was the pleasure of sitting back and delighting in listening to the superb choral singing on Sundays and during week day Evensongs. For us as canons, surrounded by the responsibilities and pressures of the parish, to be uplifted by such musicianship was an unsurpassable spiritual experience. Sadly once a canon retires from his parish his time as canon in residence ceases. However the title Canon continues.

Whenever I returned home from the canonry it took me a few days to adjust to the normal pace of parish routine after the rarefied air of St. Davids. It was a little like coming down to the valley of service after being for a while on the Mount of Transfiguration. Not that one does not need both in the life of a servant of Christ. During our first year in the parish, Gwendoline arranged a visit by a group of forty from both our churches to enjoy a guided tour of the cathedral and receive a prepared tea at the canonry which is located in the cathedral close. They were all able to appreciate why those who come to St. Davids come as pilgrims and not just as visitors, because here visitors discover a building and a setting quite unique and set apart. Gwendoline and I were glad to have a hand with the washing up this time!

One more surprise came my way before the end of our time in the parish. In 2006 I celebrated my sixty fifth birthday. As I was given to understand, the close family were joining for a meal at the Gwenllian Hotel in Cydweli. I should have known better! As I opened the door of the dining room, a gathering of some sixty guests were there to greet me! Gwendoline had done it again – bless her! It was a truly convivial evening which, once I had taken it all in, was much enjoyed by us all.

The following year I decided that with the completion of the Llandyry Restoration Project and having passed my sixty sixth birthday, it was timely to call it a day. I had received the benefit of competent and hard-working churchwardens who eased many burdens from my shoulders and officers who showed great commitment in serving their parish well. What incumbent would not have valued the compiling of the kind of weekly newsletter that Wendy, our secretary, brought out faithfully without being asked to do so? A newsletter is such an essential means of contact between church and community and a God-send to those who are house-bound. For the same reason I arranged a monthly newsletter at Llandyry for their benefit.

Being incumbent of this parish had been an eventful and busy last chapter of parochial ministry, blessed by warm and constructive relationships between priest and congregations and between both congregations themselves. I think that we accomplished much together in the space of just over 6 years. As my ministerial ship came into its haven of rest in June 2007, I looked back with satisfaction on this last lap of the voyage as being a period of working together in harmony as captain, crew and passengers, to ensure that the vessel came into port in fine fettle. Throughout this last stage of my pilgrimage I had the full support of my wife to help me face the daily routine and to be someone in whom I could implicitly confide. The generosity of spirit extended to me personally throughout my incumbency was borne out in the kind farewell gifts of a lap top and hostess trolley for Gwendoline and myself to appreciate in our retirement. As someone who had had so many dealings with the maintenance of churches in my care it was, I suppose, gratifying to come into the final harbour having savoured the atmosphere of two churches whose long history went back centuries after years of dealing with buildings of the Victorian age.

CHAPTER 10

FROM DESOLATION TO NATIONAL TREASURE

In Chapter 6 I described the appalling state in which we found "the ancient church on the marsh" when we visited the site on Christmas Day 1975. Bearing in mind the fact that the church eventually took on the profile of a building of national significance, I want to trace here the unique thread of this story of a phoenix rising from

Llandeilo Talybont church, sited at
St. Fagan's Museum, Cardiff

the ashes. I have decided to follow the saga here at the point of my retirement because its "complete make-over" was officially acclaimed and therefore acted as an unforgettable completion to my parish ministry in the autumn of 2007. Let us recap in order to put the whole story in perspective.

Up until about twenty five years ago, those of us travelling east from Exit 48 on the M4 would have been able to see on the left of the motorway a lime-washed church, bounded by a circular churchyard wall (the round shape being an indication of antiquity) located on a slight rise just within forty yards of the eastern bank of the River Loughor. This building of rather ordinary appearance was the parish church of Llandeilo Talybont, the ecclesiastical name for the parish that comprises Pontarddulais. There are a few "bridges" in the vicinity that may suggest to the reader the derivation of the "Pont" or "Bont" in both these names. We can of course discount the stretch of motorway and the railway line that spans the River Loughor at this point, (as this dates from the 19th century), whereas the church is several centuries older. No! This is the "bridge" that crosses a tributary of the Loughor, called the Dulais. This bridge is seen as you enter Pontarddulais from the village of Hendy. (Traffic lights have been installed on the road near this bridge during recent years) For the meaning of Llandeilo Talybont, therefore read "the church of Saint Teilo beyond the bridge". The description of its location was intended primarily for those travelling along the River Loughor towards its estuary. These travellers would have regarded the church as the next landmark after passing under the Dulais Bridge. After all it was mainly by boat that worshippers made their way to the church for centuries.

For many years services had been held at the church once a month during the summer and at Easter and Harvest. After the last Harvest Festival held there the guest preacher caught pneumonia and, sadly, later died. Services were limited to afternoons because there was no electricity. The last service was held there in 1970 after which the church was abandoned for worship. By then it was recognised that the building was deteriorating fast, due to its location which made it vulnerable to the prevailing south-westerly winds coming from the river estuary, and to the increasing vandalism which had resulted in the theft of lead from the roof and breakings in. The latter allowed animals as well as humans to wander in at will and wreak havoc. The church's remoteness made it virtually impossible to maintain vigilance to prevent wanton damage or monitor storm damage. The nearest habitation was a farm dwelling some 250 yards away and the nearest point of access by car was about a quarter of a mile distant. The problems were exacerbated by evidence of "devil worship" during the 1960's. As mentioned in an earlier chapter, the chaos that greeted our eyes when my first wife and I first visited the church in 1975 was indescribable. Pews had been wrenched away from the floor and stood at an angle. Books had been left ripped in untidy heaps, urine and excrement, both animal and human, were spattered about everywhere and curtains behind doors left in disarray. It was a scene of utter destruction that could well have been a film set from World War 2. Clearly things could not continue as they were. Some long-term solution had to be found for the "church on the marsh."

For several years the parish was in consultation with the diocesan authorities concerning the situation and was also in correspondence with a body known as "The Friends of Friendless Churches." The latter was known for its support for every effort made by parishes who had responsibility for remote and vulnerable church buildings. But how to find a permanent solution? Two ideas presented themselves. The first solution would be to eliminate possible damage and vandalism by removing all interior furniture and fabrics and dismantling the roof completely, leaving just the external walls, so that visitors would see an interesting semi-ruin, much like Tintern Abbey in the Wye Valley or St. Dogmael's Abbey near Cardigan. Suitable plaques would be placed at strategic points along the walls pointing out the features as visitors toured the site. Thus it could turn out to be a serious contender for the tourists' hotspots! Attractive and reasonable though this idea appeared, and excited with the prospect of being able to showcase the ancient church to visitors though we would be, this idea, on reflection seemed a little "pie in the sky." After all, how many people would be resolute enough, let alone fit enough, to venture across the fields from either the nearest access point by car under the present motorway at Waungron, or risk the constant tidal movement of the river and "slog it" along the muddy approach through the marshes from Pontarddulais itself, - just to view a semi-ruin? And there would be no refreshments or toilet facilities at the end of their onerous journey, or any steward to welcome them there. No! There had to be an alternative! This is where the second idea was mooted. (By yours truly I have to say). Could the church be rebuilt somewhere else where it could be seen to advantage?

I had been informed on good authority that beneath the plaster work on the walls of the church impressive murals were hidden but that these murals had been the victim of a "cover up" during the period of the Reformation when it was deemed inappropriate to have such colourful items adorning the House of God. The thought came to me, "What if we were to uncover part of the walls and find out more about these reputed murals? It was with this in mind that I contacted the Glamorgan and Gwent Archaeological Society, who confirmed that there was every indication that murals were in existence. We decided that, under the supervision of the diocesan architect, the archaeologists should undertake an exploratory survey of the walls. What they managed to uncover left firm evidence that here were some very impressive late medieval murals. My first thought was to contact the Curator of the Museum of Welsh Life at St. Fagan's to find out if our church might therefore be of interest to the Museum. I explained that we had an abandoned building dating from the early fifteenth century in need of urgent restoration with the prospect of revealing unique murals but which equally urgently needed a new permanent address! I had a very warm response to my enquiry. It was agreed in principle to take down the church stone by stone and faithfully re-erect it in the National Museum at St. Fagan's where it would be completely restored to be viewed as it would have appeared in the early part of the sixteenth century, that is, just before the Reformation. However it would take more than twenty years to take this plan from the drawing board to actual implementation.

Sad to say, much time was spent during the 1980's and right up to 1992 establishing legal rights of passage

to enable the building to be taken down and painstak-
ingly removed through the fields adjacent to the church
so that it could begin life in its new home. After a long
legal wrangle about access with a neighbouring farmer
was over, and only then, could the restoration start in
earnest. The enormity and uniqueness of this project
should not be underestimated. This was the first time
that such an ancient church had been removed to an
open air museum in Great Britain. Though some
churches have been rebuilt in museums on the Conti-
nent, these have been timber-built whereas the church
of Llandeilo Talybont was constructed of solid masonry.
So, by the turn of the millennium, this church, devastated to the point of desolation, was preparing itself to
be transformed for ever into its presumed original late
medieval state where it could be admired by a nation.

Although the church is believed to have been built
originally during the thirteenth century on the site of
an earlier pre-Norman church, the centuries that
followed saw much alteration and extension. Before
it was removed from the banks of the River Loughor
what you saw was a structure dating from the early
fifteenth century. During the latter part of that century,
for instance, an additional aisle was added to the south
side of the nave, as with many churches of that period.
In order to improve the congregation's view of the altar
from this side aisle, a "squint" opening was inserted
into the wall of the chancel arch. Finally an entrance
porch (almost always the most recent addition to older
churches) was added to this south aisle.

It was decided to refurbish the church as it would
have appeared about the year 1520. One of the reasons
for this choice of date was that experts in mural art had

concluded that the fine series of wall paintings that had been uncovered in 1983 dated from this time because some have been copied from illustrations in books printed in the early seventeenth century. This meant that the church in its re-constructed state in St. Fagan's represented a place of worship for those in this country who still clung to Roman Catholic faith and practice. An example of this tradition is the re-installing of the rood-screen between the nave and the chancel as a symbol of the difference in status between the role of the priest at the altar and the people in the nave. Today in our liturgy and in our design of churches we have come away from this idea of the "isolated priest up there" and the congregation distantly "down there." We now declare in our Creed, "*We* believe in God" etc. and, far from the altar being in the distance, it is often brought forward centrally to the body of the church, for all to see what is happening when the bread and the wine are consecrated. The design of the church today emphasises that we are all "together worshipping God" as one family of faith.

The main effect on the eye of the present visitor to the church now housed at St. Fagan's, in contrast with the church as I saw it first in 1975, is the stunning range of colours that hits you as you enter. This blaze of colour (some may judge it to be rather obtrusively bright) is due to the wall paintings that make the church appear to some visitors somewhat like a mini exhibition room within a sacred building. A cynic may well ask, "Why would churches have needed all these paintings? Yet we would do well to remember that church services before the Reformation were conducted in Latin which very few ordinary people understood. Wall-paintings helped to remind the congregation of the stories and messages of the Bible and the lives of the saints to encourage them to reflect while they listened. They acted as a visual aid and a focus for reflection as the service proceeded. They were painted directly on to the lime plaster which covered the walls. Often, after a generation or two, new paintings would take the place of the old ones to introduce a change of theme. Think how we like to change the décor of our homes when we need things to have a "new look". With the coming of the Reformation itself in the mid 1530's, the paintings fell out of favour and were plastered over. Later again in Victorian times, the walls were covered with whitewash thus resulting in original paintings centuries old being hidden from view beneath layer upon layer of lime wash and whitewash. The two earliest paintings in the church date from about 1400, one of which depicts Saint Catherine of Siena. The entire church seems to have been refurbished with scenes from the life of Christ round about 1500. In preparation for the re-opening of the church at St. Fagan's, stories from the life of Saint Teilo were especially commissioned to be included on the walls by modern artists, to mark the church's dedication to this saint.

It should be said that during the 1970's and the 1980's a growing number of religious buildings in Wales were becoming redundant because of declining congregations or by virtue of their being located in remote places. During this period St. Fagan's had been offered several churches for possible preservation. Saint Teilo's church at Pontarddulais met the criteria more obviously than any other. Its great virtue was that it had barely been touched by the restorers of the Victorian era, thus making it more viable for redesigning according to how it must have appeared in the late medieval period. Its saving grace was the intriguing prospect of the crumbling plaster on its walls concealing traces of early murals. As it is, to use theological terminology, what was hidden proved to be its *salvation* and, ultimately, its *resurrection*.

The restoration of the "old church" has given rise to a feeling of great pride and delight among the people of Pontarddulais and surrounding areas because their "local treasure" is now recognised as a "national treasure" which Wales can now share with the rest of the world. It is the only example of an Anglican church in the National Museum of Welsh Life, yet having said this, it is technically the only example also of a Roman Catholic place of worship. We have come a long way from the description of the church by the poet Edward Thomas, published in the book "Beautiful Wales" in 1905 in which he refers to it as "a little desolate white church with white-walled graveyard."

Every year on the feast of St. Teilo, which is February 9th parishioners of Llandeilo Talybont embark on a pilgrimage to their old parish church for a service of thanksgiving. I was pleased to join the Friends of Brecon cathedral for their annual excursion to St. Fagan's in September 2012 when they held a service in the church, led by the Dean of Brecon. I was asked to give a brief outline of the church's history during the service, which gave me great pleasure.

It would seem that at present a service can be held at the church only by special arrangement. For practical reasons I fully understand why the right to solemnise marriages has been excluded since this would inevitably lead to excessive demand for its use to the detriment of visitors coming out or interest in the normal way. However, I feel that the church should be seen to be a living place of worship as often as practicable for ordinary Sunday worship so that the worshipping heritage of the past is continued today. After all, the history of the church is a splendid example of the continuity of the Church through the ages – here we have a church of the Pre-reformation Roman Catholic faith which thereafter became an Anglican church and from the Anglican Church developed the Wesleyan Methodist movement until today when we have the Covenant for Union of churches in Wales. In fact I would view the church of Llandeilo Talybont as a focus for the unity of Christians throughout Wales that is happily located in a national venue. Mindful of this image, would it be too much to expect each year a Christmas Carol service, an Easter-Tide service, a Mid-Summer service and a Harvest service, each perhaps arranged on an ecumenical basis? This would provide four occasions in the year when everyone would be welcome to worship and tread where "the saints of old have trod." If members of the congregation are worried about the need to sit for the service (pre-Reformation churches had no seats!) people could be invited to bring their own folding chairs!

Much has been recorded of the life of St. Teilo. The problem with many of the lives of the early Celtic saints is how to separate fact from fiction. However, the most well-known "legends" surrounding his name are carved in a single piece of solid oak, namely, the rood-loft of the church in St. Fagan's. Thus we can say that in truth Llandeilo Talybont church links its history to today as its contemporary home links the present to the past in a most fascinating way.

The above saga of the church of St.Teilo has been described at this point because just a few months into my retirement from parochial duties in 2007 I received an official invitation to the official re-dedication of the church by the then Archbishop of Canterbury, the Most Revd. Rowan Williams. It was most appropriate that Archbishop Rowan should officiate at the ceremony because he himself is a product of the Diocese of Swansea and Brecon in which the church once stood. The then Bishop of Swansea and Brecon, the Rt. Revd. Anthony Pierce, was present as also was the present incumbent of Llandeilo Talybont, Canon John Walters, who succeeded me as the incumbent of the parish. I would like to commend most warmly the diligence and patience of John and his parishioners in taking the destiny of their parish church so much to heart through the tiresome years of legal hassle in order to ensure that the dream that was born during my period of ministry was strenuously pursued and finally realised in October 2007.

I cannot adequately express the deep sense of satisfaction it gave me to attend this Re-dedication Service. Here we were witnessing a tale of "from rags to riches", or more appropriately in the case of a building, a church transformed from devastation to a national treasure.

CHAPTER 11

ALL THINGS CONSIDERED

N.B.   In any reference to clergy in the masculine gender in this chapter please relate also to the feminine gender

Gwendoline and I retired to a pleasantly located bungalow in Burry Port, with chemists, surgeries, railway station (hourly service to Manchester) and even a church all within about 400 yards. One has to be practical

Sanctuary of Llandeilo Talybont church

as one gets older. Views and locations are fine but facilities are a "must". My wife, who suffers from a spinal problem, was as keen as myself in investing in a home without having to cope with stairs. (My desire stemmed from ease of maintenance of the property, whereas hers was a medical necessity). As with most people, it took me a few months to adjust to no parish responsibilities, no church meetings of an evening, and, perhaps above all, no urgent phone calls requiring my attention. The garden, which for almost all my ministry has been somewhat of a chore, consists of a small front lawn, two flower beds and a rear patio with potted plants! Our grandchildren, aged 3 and 6 respectively, keep us from becoming decrepit. There is nothing quite like engaging with children to widen and enrich your life, even if they take up a lot of your energy. It is usually energy well spent when you see one child's face light up when he can sit in the driving seat of a life-boat at Burry Port harbour and get the "feel" of being in charge and the other child's face light up when she receives a new doll and gets a "kick" out of singing her to sleep! I believe that the timing of my retirement has destined me to take full advantage of seeing them grow through their childhood – surely the best time to share their company.

What follows in this chapter is my assuming the role of an artist who paints a landscape with wide, sweeping movements of the brush as the mood dictates, listing some of the many things that have given me great satisfaction in my ministry and mentioning a few things that have caused dismay. Retirement gives one time to reflect and evaluate in a spirit of seeing things hopefully in some perspective. This is the prerogative of those who are in the comparative seclusion of the "side lines" of the main railway track while watching the trains go trundling by. Within a few months of retiring I received the inevitable enquiries about taking a Sunday service and the trend has continued ever since. They say that clergy never retire from the pitch; they just move back to the "subs' bench!" However it is good to know that retired clergy can play a part in the maintenance of parish routine, especially in these days of prolonged vacancies in parishes. Even in the normal routine of ministry, how would serving clergy cope with regard to having a holiday or how would the parish schedule continue with a parish priest off duty because of a medical problem etc. if retired clergy were not around to "fill the gap?"

The Church in Wales faces a deep crisis in its full-time ordained ministry. The number of those being ordained compares unfavourably with the number of those soon to retire. Added to this, we have the acute shortage of clergy who are able to speak Welsh. As churchgoing has declined during recent decades, so inevitably have the parishes nurturing vocations to the sacred ministry declined. This is especially true of the rural, Welsh-speaking areas where there has been an increasing migration of younger people to the more populated areas of Wales and over the border. I find now that I am being asked to officiate in Welsh twice as much as in English because of the dearth of Welsh speakers. I think that the Church in Wales should act more strategically to highlight the need for clergy who are aspiring to minister in bilingual areas to pursue a crash course in Welsh (at least for a month, preferably for three months) BEFORE taking up their appointment. This should be agreed between respective bishops, if the move is to another diocese. Once the parish priest is in post, there is little time for such a course to be taken with so many new responsibilities to face. However, as the cleric settles into the parish, further "refresher courses" would be desirable, by which time the parish priest will have become used to hearing Welsh regularly and, hopefully, taking services in Welsh in his new parish. In my experience Welsh-speaking congregations are quite sympathetic towards the difficulties facing clergy who are learning Welsh and will tolerate a sermon in English (with perhaps a few sentences in simple Welsh thrown in) as long as the service is basically in Welsh. At least Welsh is phonetic and should cause few problems to pronounce. Many clergy born and brought up in England have mastered the language surely to the embarrassment of those brought up in Wales. In a bilingual situation, the ball is firmly in the court of the "would be" parish priest to relate fully into the culture of the community in which he is to serve. But the ball is equally firmly in the court of the Church in Wales to provide incentives to meet that desire. This is a provincial problem and it requires a provincial strategy to which bishops of all dioceses in Wales should co-operate to address if bilingual parishes are to be more effectively served in future.

As I look back on my career I think how fortunate I have been in relating to and working with people of all kinds of background. The Prayer Book of 1662 has such an apt phrase to describe the wide compass in which the cleric functions; it speaks of *"all sorts and conditions of men."* (To conform with politically correct language these days please read "people" for "men".) The saying is very true that "you do not have to *like* people in order to *love* them", even though I must admit to having been baffled by the saying when I first heard it. Let me illustrate this. I confess that on a few occasions when duty has compelled me to call on a person with whom I did not relate too well, I have made my way to the door of that person's home and have earnestly prayed to the Almighty that he or she is not at home so that I could slip my visiting card through the letter box and thus avoid personal contact. Despite these uncharitable feelings towards the person concerned, this has not precluded me from dismissing from my mind Our Lord's command to *"love one another as I have loved you."* Remember that the Pharisees and the Sadducees were not always Our Lord's "flavour of the month" but can we really imagine him making an exception of these opponents of his in matters of controversy when he called his disciples to "love your enemies?" Through my thirty eight years of parish ministry I have been no exception in having my disagreements with church officers, parishioners and colleagues (even on one notable occasion with a bishop, as described in an earlier chapter) but no swords have been drawn as a result. We have begged to differ in charity. I recall one conversation with a parishioner who refused to receive the sacrament from a female Eucharistic assistant who was assisting me by administering the chalice. *"But I have consecrated the bread and the wine,"* said I, in desperation, *"so, what's the problem?"* *"Well, I don't feel it's the same somehow!"* she declared. It was as much as I could do not to "blow my top" and call her the most prejudiced person I had ever met. At moments like these, when we are provoked to harbour unkind thoughts towards others, hopefully we restrain our frustration and in the name of Christ continue to love these people whose opinions we may object to.

The great privilege of the parish priest is that he is called to serve people where they are, as they are. He can knock on the door of any stranger in the parish and introduce himself thus," Hello! Good to see you. I'm your vicar." While you have to register with a General Practitioner and you have to call in a solicitor of your choice, the ordained ministry is the only profession in which the ordained person has a claim on any parishioner, even though many are unaware of that claim or dispute it for some deep-seated reason. This said, clergy are to be distinguished from social workers, for instance. I recall an ordinand's reaction to an assignment set by his tutor in Pastoral Studies at St. Michaels' College during my time there. The topic set was "How would you approach a conversation with a parishioner who had recently been informed that he had a terminal condition?" The ordinand's response was, "Who does he think we are - ruddy social workers?" Social workers address their expertise towards individuals and families who are in a certain known category of need or hardship, whether it be social deprivation, domestic violence or safeguarding of children or adults. By contrast, the priest makes himself available to any person, whatever the need may be. True- the majority of reasons for most people desiring contact with clergy is that they have a specific task for the priest to carry out, - a funeral, a christening or a wedding come easiest to mind. But our calling as clergy is not limited to those areas of our profession which those outside the Church are most likely to believe are our sole responsibility. (The old chestnut about clergy working on Sundays only and at funerals!) Many a time I have read out a letter sent to a partially sighted person or made a cup of tea for those whose rheumatoid arthritis prevents them from making it themselves or telephoned a chemist on behalf of someone with dementia to make sure that the person has received tablets of the correct strength. These, and countless more, are examples of clergy seeing there and then opportunities for ministry, simply by being in the right place at the right time, rather than the social worker, for example, who is detailed to address a specific need known about beforehand. I remember vividly being at the hospital bedside of Elsie Jenkins whose life was slowly ebbing away. However her mental powers were still intact. A young trainee nurse came up to the bedside armed with a clipboard containing a checklist to be filled in with regard to the patient's medications, intake of fluids etc. which needed the co-operation of the patient for replies. The trainee nurse went methodically through the list, ticking the boxes while looking steadfastly down at her clipboard as the patient responded as best she could. After about two or three minutes, I could not restrain myself any longer. I dared to say, *"Nurse, Elsie has a face as well as a name!"* I might equally have said, *"And her face might tell you as much as the checklist!"* I am sure that this nurse would eventually make a competent and caring professional person but my comment was intended to help her see that her vocation depended on how she related to her patient on a human level. The data on the checklist belonged to a person whose name was Elsie. Without this human dimension they were just data to be fed into a computer.

For similar reasons I am most irritated when I enter the room of a G.P. and, on entering, what greets me is the sight of the doctor's eyes glued to the screen of the computer. No handshake or smile of welcome, just *"Good morning, please sit down"*, with no move to look in my direction. I realise that people have their job to do and are often under great stress to cope with its demands, but are we so controlled by this technological age that the face of the person with whom we are dealing commands less attention than the computer screen? When the human touch is at work, there is a confidence, a trust at work and the desire to confide in the person whose help one is seeking. I hope and pray that the Church will not lose sight of the human dimension in its mission. If it does, it will surely be in terminal decay.

Of course we know that dealing with human beings can be a risky business. When we introduce ourselves on the doorstep we may receive a storm of verbal abuse or a stiff upper-lip response like, *"Thank you, but no cold callers today!"* But at least we have succeeded in making face-to-face contact. We can leave a prayer card or contact details so that the person visited can match name to face. We leave the rest to God to work his purpose out with that person. The pastor has to be patient. The farmer can only sow the seed and hope that in good time it bears fruit. But the challenge to make ourselves "available" is one that cannot be avoided. Similarly, when we seek to help those with a particular anxiety either about themselves or someone close to them, we are not in the business of parading as instant miracle-workers who by referring to a verse of Scripture can address the problem successfully. I well remember a young curate in the deanery in which I was serving at the time being left to "hold the fort" in the parish while his vicar was on holiday and was confronted with taking the funeral of a child. He was nervous enough to ask my advice. I commended him for his courage in admitting that help was needed. My advice was to "be yourself and avoid glib phrases that give the impression that "all is well if you keep your faith in God". It is better to say "I stand alongside you in your grief, no words of mine can adequately express how devastated you must be at this time – but Jesus suffered too and knows what you as a family are going through." We are called to be alongside the needy person and not on the other side of the "professional desk". People who are bereaved need a "prop" to lean on, not a recipe for overcoming their grief. All this is made easier when we see the pastoral situation at a human level, seeing the bereaved person's needs as a whole and helping that person face his guilt or pain or loneliness without advocating neat ways of solving difficult problems.

One of our basic assets as clergy should be practising the art of listening before being ready to talk. One of the greatest compliments we can be paid is to receive the response, "Thanks anyway for listening to my problems. Just to talk to someone is a help." Being there to hear them pour out their anxieties is all that is perhaps required at the time. "Being there for them" is the all-important thing, not any pre-conceived theory of how we can help rid them of their worries. Talking through the situation with the sufferer is a ministry to be prized and then having the tactfulness to withdraw, if only for a while, when the sufferer claims his space before taking the next step on his own with God's help.

One of my favourite episodes in the Gospels is found only in the Gospel of Mark and it is the incident of the woman with a haemorrhage who is brave enough to touch the hem of Christ's robe as the crowd jostle their way to catch a glimpse of Jesus. What happened is incidental to the narrative of the Gospel at the time but it is a very significant detail for pondering priorities in ministry. Jesus turns and confronts the sufferer whom he recognises has sought contact with him. He makes her spell out her problem, reluctant though she is to make any undue fuss. She would have preferred help "by remote control", so as to avoid public attention drawn to herself but the help comes through a person to person encounter, even midst the hubbub all around. Is there a drift into a less than human approach into which the Church at large is in danger of slipping? Are we finding it easier in this age of the email and the twitter to deal with situations by remote control instead of face to face? I am not for a moment decrying the advantages of cyberspace as a means of valid communication when required. But can it be that we are looking for more indirect ways that perhaps save us time and energy but run the risk of a less personal form of dealing with the problems people face? This point struck me most forcibly some years before my retirement when our bishop spoke most eloquently about the positive benefits that the Church might receive from consulting with a senior Market Research officer for the retail firm Tesco. If it had not been a more weighty matter on my conscience, I would have laughed in derision at the idea. Can Tesco or any other commercial enterprise possibly reveal anything worthwhile about the mission of the Church in this day and age? One body is committed to offering the public what they most *desire* and the other Body is committed to offering people what they most *need*. Is the Church so concerned with cash flow problems that it turns to commerce for possible answers? The answer to financial stresses besetting the church is surely to be found at a less materialistic level that involves us in the whole question of our responsibility as Christian stewards.

As I drew nearer to retirement I found that the Church resorted more and more to questionnaires based on sociological issues, such as percentage of unemployment in the parish, social deprivation, children in care etc. These were relevant enough to our work up to a point, but what outcomes came from them? What benefit did the filling in of such questionnaires give the Church except to say that such and such a survey had been made and these findings were noted? Just another "checklist" completed, just another load of data for the computer to digest, just another example of bureaucracy, as far as I can judge. Call me a cynic in my senior age, if you like!

Clergy Review is doing the rounds at present. This process is intended to offer professional support to clergy. When I was submitted to this Review it seemed to me, at the age of 63, that either I was to be considered beyond the need for such support because my retirement was pending or else I had shown myself to be so inadequate professionally that it would be sensible to treat me by then as a lost cause. Being charitable, perhaps the Church needed to evaluate clergy at every step of their career and my age-group had to be represented. There was a huge questionnaire to be completed ranging from the nature of the parish for which one is responsible, the domestic circumstances of the priest, the attitude to parish work, the range of duties one undertakes, contact with various age-groups etc. After completing this questionnaire, the responses are discussed with a mentor (one of the senior staff of the diocese) and a written report is received by the priest. Apart from some very positive and pleasing comments about my general professional conduct and commitment to my duties, a number of points that I raised of concern to me produced little or no feed-back in the report. Were they destined for oblivion? As my own sights were fixed on retirement in a short time this did not unduly trouble me, but if I had been a cleric starting out in ministry or in middle years, I would have felt let down by this apparent lack of "follow-up". So the question I ask is - given that clergy, like teachers, need constant professional and personal support, however experienced they may be – what outcomes flow from this pattern of Clergy Review? The question remains – Are we becoming so eager to emulate other professions in terms of good practice, management skills and aids to promote a "sharper edge" to our effectiveness as priestly and pastoral practitioners that we are in danger of throwing out the baby with the bath water? Has the Church the resources to begin to match that which is being done to support professional standards in the classroom, for instance? If we are serious about this important issue, why not arrange for a suitably qualified person in each archdeaconry, under the personal supervision of the archdeacon, to act as "mentor" to the clergy in professional matters and especially in the field of personal support where there is an emotional problem such as stress, isolation, illness or bereavement besetting the cleric or any member of his/her family. The role of that mentor would be to act as a critical friend (with the accent on "friend") who is there to listen and observe, give advice if necessary and pass on matters for urgent attention to the archdeacon. If conducted sensitively and in strict confidence, such a pattern would at least have the advantage of a "person to person" approach in which needs and difficulties could be talked through and this in itself can be a healing and wholesome process. I appreciate the Church's commitment over the past 15 years or so to Continuing Ministerial Education, but this process engages with the professional development of all clergy as a group of professionals and not as individuals with their own special needs. I urge the Church to avoid losing sight of its traditional image of having a human face and, in so doing, reject the de-humanising trend of so many institutions of today.

I was informed by a retired colleague recently that those training for the ordained ministry today are advised to use their discretion about contemplating visiting parishioners in a "one-to-one" situation. This advice is given naturally for the cleric's own protection. If this is so, one may ask, "How would G.P.'s, community nurses and other home visitors apply similar discretion?" This cautionary advice is understandable if the person to be visited is someone with a known record of violence or emotional instability, but surely putting a lid on visiting all and sundry unless the priest is accompanied is to forfeit the unique privilege of his being vulnerable in his role as a "friend of the friendless." A fatal incident occurred several years ago in which a parish priest in the diocese of Llandaff was attacked verbally and then viciously stabbed to death on his doorstep. This was a sudden, unforeseeable tragedy but it might well have weighed heavily with Church authorities as to the safety of clergy issue. Yes! We must be sensible and take precautions but "safety first at all costs" for all circumstances would seem to be too drastic. I believe that the watchword on this vulnerability matter should be, "Dare to venture in ministry but be sensible in the daring!"

Dramatic changes have taken place during the past 50 years to change the whole concept of the work of the parish priest. Before I was ordained there was an aura about the status of the parson which made him feel a little like being king of his castle. There are still those clergy who would think along those feudal lines today and speak arrogantly about "my parish" and "no confetti to be thrown in my churchyard!" etc. There are no scriptural or doctrinal grounds for taking this self-appointed "lord of all I survey" attitude. It is archaic and is in complete denial of the example of humble service shown by Jesus's washing of the disciples' feet at the Last Supper. In those days of clergy domination over their flock the priest may have wielded more power but he was essentially an isolated figure. He stood or fell by his own actions. During recent decades however the priest has acquired a different role - that of a team leader, an enabler and a sensitive delegator. This new role has not come about through necessity of circumstances but by conviction that it is of God and commended by Our Lord's example of gathering together a team of disciples and "sending them out". The parish priest points to a way forward and the team discuss the wisdom of this suggestion so that, once a team decision is made, everyone in that team is supportive and all hold responsibility for its success or failure. When I was an adviser in the field of vocations I liked to compare the parish priest's role to that of a head teacher in a school. The head teacher is ultimately responsible for the defining ethos of that school but relies on all the staff to see that the values and priorities, agreed as a vision shared by all, are demonstrated. The image of a conductor of an orchestra is also useful. The players in the orchestra take their cue from the conductor. He brings the instruments in at the right time; he brings cohesion to bear on the scene but, at the same time, if left on his own without the orchestra, no musical sound can be heard. The rich music that delights our ears is only possible when conductor and players unite to display their respective talents under his direction. So through the years the cleric has progressed from a "Lone Ranger", doing his own thing, to a "Team Player", guiding and empowering those in his care.

I would like now to share with you the characteristics of clergy who have influenced me for good in my ministry and take this opportunity of expressing my indebtedness to them. Some of them I have known well, others I have admired at a distance. Each one had different talents but all of them in their various ways pointed me towards the God of our salvation.

The first incumbent of my home parish that I have any memory of was George Shilton Evans who had arrived before World War 2 and retired in 1949 to live outside Weston–Super-Mare. My boyhood memories of him revolve mainly around Sunday school parties because Shilton Evans was usually the star attraction by entertaining us with his monologues. The dramatic way he narrated the story of *"John stood on the burning deck"* is still with me, complete with thick, bushy eyebrows that went up and down with the emotional cadences demanded by the gripping story. He was undoubtedly an actor of some talent and, nurtured in the Evangelical tradition, his natural gift for "gripping his audience" made for some fiery proclaiming of the Gospel from the pulpit. I was too young to appreciate the substance of his sermons but I recall the great conviction with which he spoke. It contained what perhaps is sometimes missing from our preaching today – the capacity to move people emotionally as well as intellectually. We read how St. John, in his description of the Christian churches to whom he writes in the Book of Revelation, reserves much criticism for the church at Laodicea whose faith is "luke-warm." You could never accuse Shilton of the shortcomings of Laodicea in that respect! His manner was so intense that you were either carried away by its fervent flow or you shivered at the knees in case you were caught out failing to be convinced by what he said! Of course this was inevitably from the standpoint of a child at the time. A great character, but one whose popular appeal within much of the Anglican Church was now perhaps coming to an end. He came to be our guest preacher at the Centenary Celebratory services of St. Catherine's in 1968 at the age of 91 and, apart from the fact that his voice was, understandably, more frail, the robust vitality of his message still held his congregation. His compassion for those suffering during the Nazi obscenities of the War apparently prompted him to make many political statements denouncing tyranny. He was, above all, a great pastor of his people. If Mrs Jones was a regular worshipper and she missed attending on Sunday morning for no known reason he would take the trouble to call on her on Monday to find out what was wrong. Every Christmastide he personally distributed ten shillings discreetly to those in financial adversity in the parish. This reminds me of the truth that the effective preacher is the effective pastor, whatever his churchmanship.

In 1950 we welcomed John Richards as our vicar – the self-same man who had served his title in the parish of Pembrey and had gone abroad under the auspices of one of the missionary societies to Persia (now called Iran) with such a fine reputation that he was fondly nick-named "The Shah of Persia" on his return. John Richards had little of his predecessor's "dramatics" but did possess a very crisp, forthright delivery. I was beginning to take more notice of clergy's mannerisms by now and I must say that he certainly kept my attention with his no-nonsense style. Indeed his reputation for "take it or leave it" outspokenness divided the parish (so I was later informed) into two camps – supporters and objectors. I believe that this was much the mixed response that he seemed to elicit as a bishop later in his ministry. Perhaps his favourite saying of Christ was, "*He that is not with me is against me.*" There is no doubt that he was the sort who would not suffer fools gladly but on the other hand knew the clear direction in which he was going and wished others to go. I remember him being well received by us boys at the grammar school when he came to speak in our school assembly about his missionary exploits. I think that his robust style of speaking held the attention of young people where a milder, more inoffensive speaker would have struggled to win us over. One description of John Richards that would not suit would be "bland!" Perhaps working in the mission field of a largely Muslim country had the effect of moulding his very direct approach to the Christian faith. He stayed in Pontypridd only four and a half years before being appointed Dean of Bangor and thence Bishop of St. Davids. I felt at the time that here was someone destined for high office. He had that air of authority and "gravitas" that one expects from our "fathers in God." Thus the first two parish priests that made their mark on me certainly had distinctive marks of personality to leave!

In 1954 Stanley Mogford arrived at St. Catherine's. Stan was the parish priest who most influenced my gradually developing interest in the life of the Church. I was now much more conscious of what the Church stood for and my convictions were slowly being formed about the truth of the Gospel. Stan went to Oxford to study for his academic qualifications and trained for the ministry at Westcott House, Cambridge. He may have been born and brought up in South Wales but he spoke like an Oxford don! His was a very smooth, measured, listenable voice that was more suited to the description of a "teaching preacher", - one might well say that he was more in line with the communicators of today's Church. The reason for my emphasis on these clergy as performers in the pulpit and not in other aspects of their ministry is that it is in preaching that the personality of the cleric becomes most pronounced and it is as *personalities* that I was most in their debt regarding their influencing me at the time. Also it was on Sundays and not in the humdrum of parish routine that I saw them in action! It was during Stan's tenure of office that

I was prepared for confirmation at the age of 15. By then I was definitely committed to a living faith even though my mind was still bent on a teaching career. I suppose that it was the teaching instinct in me that drew me to Stan's capacity to communicate the Word so lucidly, movingly and attractively. Of all the many occasions I had "sat at his feet" the most memorable moments were his Lenten addresses. He used to sit in relaxed mode in the "bishop's chair" at the chancel step and the Scriptural and Church teaching just flowed from him. For me as a teenager this was riveting stuff. It was Stan who wrote my first testimonial for me when I successfully applied for my first teaching post at Bishop of Llandaff High school. By now I was a Lay Reader for which office he recommended me. Stan moved on to become Rector of Llanblethian with Cowbridge in 1963. He was Clerical Secretary of the Llandaff Diocesan Conference for many years and a Canon of Llandaff Cathedral. He was a man of wide scholarship, articulate, possessing a balanced frame of mind and, above all, he was a profoundly humble priest, with no ambitions to seek any higher office. He lived until almost attaining his 100th birthday, devotedly cared for by his wife, Joyce, during his last years. He retained an amazing memory recall and the ability to write to his friends almost right to the end.

Of course my home parish had a curate working with the vicar and of these I want to select for mention Kenneth Price. Ken and his wife Hilda and I had followed each other around! After an incumbency at Creunant, Ken became Vicar of St. Fagan, Aberdare by which time I was teaching at the local grammar school there. One of my pupils was Ken's son, Wynne. When

I went to be vicar of Pontarddulais, my first wife, Sheila, taught Ken's daughter, Mary, at Gorseinon, Ken then being the Vicar of Pennard on Gower. Thus Ken was more than just a passing curate in my home parish when I was growing up. He served under John Richards and Stan Mogford, later becoming my predecessor but one in Aberdare. Ken was a man of high intellect, good powers of communication and was a compassionate parish priest. He ended his ministry at Morriston as a Canon Residentiary of Brecon Cathedral. Sadly he was taken ill soon after retiring and the retirement that he and Hilda so thoroughly deserved to share was not to be. Ken was a good friend and offered me wise counsel at various times in my ministry.

Of those whom I have not known personally quite so well but who have influenced my way of thinking I should mention Canon Tom Pritchard who was Vicar of Penygraig in the Rhondda and Rural Dean of Rhondda for many years. Canon Pritchard was a native of North Wales come south. I mention him particularly because he chaired the meetings of the Lay Readers' Association of the Rhondda Deanery when I was functioning as a Reader and in that role we as Readers learned so much from his grasp of theological insights. I well remember a splendid paper he gave us on the basic differences between the Catholic and Protestant traditions. This helped me greatly as my exploring of the Faith developed towards ordination. Canon Pritchard, as Rural Dean, was also instrumental in arranging for me to take services as a Reader in the churches of the Rhondda which gave me valuable experience for later.

Edwin Davies, former Vicar of Llantrisant and then St. John the Baptist in the centre of Cardiff, was known throughout Wales as the weekly writer of "Weekend Thought" in the Saturday edition of the "Western Mail". These writings were full of profound reflections expressed in a homely style for the average reader. I well recall one dashing headline to his article one week, *"The C. of E. in retreat"* Most readers would be encouraged to read on to find out what drama was now befalling the Church! Actually it was Edwin's perceptive way of introducing the benefits of spending a retreat! As vicar of Llantrisant he was a member of our deanery chapter of Pontypridd when I was a curate and I became an admirer of his wise words, gentle humour and complete lack of pomposity. I have seldom heard a more thought-provoking Three hours' devotional service on Good Friday than one he conducted in Pontypridd when I was a Reader – again at a time when I would have been encouraged in deciding for ordination. It was Edwin who was selected to champion the cause of the proposals to re-unite Anglicans and Wesleyan Methodists at the Llandaff Diocesan Day Conference in 1968. It was a losing battle that he fought against the strong Anglo-Catholic element that predominated at that time in Llandaff but one had to admire his passionate appeal that the two churches return to their original one Anglican fold. Of course the big stumbling block which caused the eventual Governing Body proposals to be defeated was the theological approach to the reciprocal ordination of Methodist ministers and Anglican clergy. Still the process led to the Covenanting Churches in Wales being set up in 1976 which strongly contends for greater understanding between churches today. I always felt that Edwin's great talents as a communicator and his charisma of personality were not fully tapped by the Church he served so well.

During more recent years I must mention a married couple who were most supportive to me during Sheila's illness and after my bereavement, Bishop Ivor Rees and wife, Beverley. Just a day or so after we received the devastating news of the diagnosis, Bishop Ivor came to see me to commiserate and show his deep concern for us. A few years after their retirement to Uzmaston, I by then being widowed, they very kindly offered me overnight accommodation during my time inspecting Merlin's Bridge school near Haverfordwest to save me a long journey home and they were homeliness itself in their hospitality. Both of them made you feel you were among true friends whenever you met them.

I mention here fleeting glimpses of two characters from across the border who made an immediate impression on me. In 1972 Archbishop Michael Ramsey addressed the Llandaff Diocesan Conference. Despite his rather eccentric appearance and mannerisms he came across as one of the most deeply spiritual leaders of the Church of England in our generation. His every word had that ring of "spiritual truth" about it that could not fail to captivate all who heard him. It was his call to the Church of England Synod to keep a period of silence and not give way to either showing signs of support or of dismay at the Anglican-Methodist vote being lost that displays his statesmanlike quality. I think he was a unique figure of his time but I would judge that Rowan Williams later emulated him as a man of outstanding spiritual calibre as archbishop.

A leading figure in the Church of England about whom I had heard but had never seen in the flesh until he came to St. Mary's Church, Swansea in 1981 was Canon David Watson. I had been very inspired by his devotional books, "In search of God", "My God is real" and "Discipleship". What struck me about these books was the way in which the ordinary person of the pew could easily turn to them and derive much blessing. His material had a rich theological basis but the theology he expounded was "applied theology", much more to be treasured in my view than "pure theology." As an acclaimed evangelist who had made such a name for himself in St. Michael-Le-Belfrey in York, I half expected a flamboyant English version of Billy Graham! How inaccurate are many of our pre-conceived ideas! I immediately saw that his appeal was due to his matter-of-fact, lucid way of presenting the Gospel, as though he was calling on his congregation to listen to the "Ten o'clock News" but of course – it was News with a difference! I have not heard anyone share God's truth with others in such a cogent, "unspectacular" way. His presentation was the more striking simply because it lacked the shallowness of an extrovert. His last book, "Fear no evil", written when he was close to death, is a living testimony to his undying faith. What a tragedy that he was lost to the Church with so much more to contribute to its life and witness.

If there was one single event that finally persuaded me to seek ordination after much heart-searching it was the week arranged ecumenically to celebrate the 400 years since the Publishing of the New Testament in Welsh by William Salisbury in 1567. The week, spent in Aberystwyth, was called "Wythnos Y Gair" (The Week of the Word"). We had worship at Llanbadarn Fawr church, workshops on the themes of Evangelism and

Discipleship in the morning, (afternoons were free) and then there were preaching services to end the day. The speakers included Bishop Mervyn Stockwood whose theme was "The Social Gospel" and the Revd. John Stott of All Souls, Langham Place whose theme was "The Personal Gospel." The then Bishop of St. Davids, Bishop John Richards (my former vicar), concluded the week's activities with an exemplary display of the art of preaching a truly bilingual address. It is no easy task to glide from one language to another without repeating yourself excessively yet developing your material cogently. It was a satisfying climax to an exciting week with opportunities to meet Christians of every denomination, some of whom I came to know later as colleagues in ministry.

The Week of the Word in Aberystwyth was an opportunity for all churches in Wales to celebrate a treasure common to them all through the centuries – The word of God. Since being actively engaged in the Christian Faith I have always been enthusiastic about the way churches should be seen to be united in fellowship and, wherever possible, in worship. I have been blessed by the support of other clergy and ministers in building relationships of mutual understanding and enterprise in parishes in which I have served. Was it not Abbé Courtier, the prime initiator of the Week of Prayer for Christian Unity, who declared "To love one another we must know one another, to know one another we must meet one another". One of the most memorable experiences I ever had in the field of Christian Unity was while attending a Roman Catholic High School's annual carol service in Llanelli about 15 years ago. I was attending in my role as a governor of the school, representing the clergy of our deanery. (The school had an intake of about 50% non-Catholic pupils). Just before the last carol was due to be sung, the R.C. priest of the parish turned to me and said, *"Would you like to pronounce the Blessing at the end?"* It was a great privilege and showed clearly what progress has been made over recent decades in the matter of greater love through greater contact between Christians. Never does this point come home to me more clearly than now in retirement when I am asked to take services in some of our Non-conformist churches. One special honour is to preside occasionally in a Wesleyan Methodist church at the Holy Communion, using the Rite of the Covenanted Churches. It is incredible how similar the Liturgy of the Sacrament is for the Roman Catholic Mass, the Anglican Eucharist and the Wesleyan Methodist Holy Communion service. The structure follows the same basic pattern. Like so many things in life, by taking more notice of the presentation rather than the substance of liturgy, we conclude that there is more distance between churches than there is in reality. Young people can often teach us a lesson here. Those young people who are keen to explore what being a Christian means do not think of using labels like Anglican, Baptist, Roman Catholic. They are content with the statement, "I am a Christian." The divided Church of Christ is as old as the era of the first Christians of course and prompted the Apostle Paul to vent his frustration on the Christians at Corinth when exhorting them to agree with one another in Christ, by saying *"Is Christ divided?"* (The meaning behind this being, *"Surely not!"*)

There is the well-known prayer of the cynically minded Christian, "Lord, give us unity, but not now!"

We fear being moved from the familiar; we resist a deviation from the usual, especially as we get older! In this context perhaps this quotation can guide our thoughts, *"The Holy Spirit comforts the disturbed, but also disturbs the comfortable"*. When we have the courage to pull up the drawbridges and let traffic flow in and out of the castle strongholds we find that the Church can move forward with renewed vigour, armed with what God can do with us together in unity. It is good to know that the work of the ecumenical "Gathering" which met recently in Aberystwyth and aspires to creating a Uniting Church in Wales, bringing together the Church in Wales, the Methodists, Presbyterians, United Reformed Church and covenanting Baptists, is gathering momentum and commands overwhelming support by the Governing Body. One hopes that this is a catalyst for things to come in the field of Christian Unity in Wales.

If I have learned one thing in ministry the hard way, it is not to take ourselves too seriously. Smiling at our own inadequacies, laughing at our own folly can restore us to a more healthy sense of proportion. Sometimes we give the clear impression that our faith is more of a burden than a blessing. *"Do not look dismal, as the hypocrites do"*, says Jesus. I am sure there was much fun and laughter at the Marriage Feast in Cana that Jesus and his disciples attended. I am sure also that there was a smile on the faces of those who heard Jesus say in a bantering tone, *"It is easier for a camel to go through the eye of a needle than for a rich man to enter the kingdom of God"*.

A sense of humour is a precious example of God's bountiful gifts to us and there is every reason why it should not be excluded from the Christian's make-up, any more than a non-Christian's. Teachers will know how much impact a humorous remark can have when a tense situation in a classroom needs to be diffused. This is true for the cleric chairing a meeting when "daggers are drawn" over some matter of consequence on the agenda. A smile brought to the face at the right time can allow for a sense of stepping back and weighing up the situation with the heat off. Nevertheless, sarcastic comments are not in this category. I well remember being a victim of sarcasm in a six - form class (astonishingly!) when the teacher made some "quirky" joke during the reading of a French novel, He directed the attention of the whole group to me, saying, *"Look at Alan, he looks as sober as a judge!"* It was not my fault that I could not see anything in what he said that was genuinely funny! Humour should never be a reason for one-upmanship! It should be guaranteed to raise the spirits of all who are present. "To laugh *with* one another" is the essence of true humour. Life for me would be intolerable without looking for the humorous in as many situations as I can.

Humour comes easily when similar words of different meaning are mixed up. A pupil in my class in Bishop of Llandaff School wrote eloquently about "how enjoyable it was to see "the monkeys on Caldey Island in their long robes!" What a school trip that must have been!

It is so easy for us as clergy to trip over words that sound alike when taken together. In the old days when churches regularly recited the 10 Commandments before the Confession at the Eucharist according to the 1662 service, I recall declaring blithely, "Thou shalt not covet thy neighbour's wife, nor his manservant, nor his maidservant, nor his axe, nor his "'oss", nor anything that is thy neighbour's". (Had I been seeing too many Western cowboy films for my own good?)

I was staggered at a wedding rehearsal once to see the father of the bride arriving 15 minutes late only to sit down without any apology and not even taking his cap off! He remained attired in cap for the remainder of the rehearsal. I was minded to tell him a few home truths immediately. However, I judged that a humorous remark with a sting to it would produce a better result. Thus before we concluded the rehearsal I placed my hand firmly on the man's shoulder and said, *"And this "gentleman" has promised me that he will not be wearing his cap in church on the day of the wedding."*

Even during the finalising of funeral arrangements an element of humour can creep in. The deceased person was passionately fond of the music of Ivor Novello. The husband expressed a wish to have her favourite song of his played on tape at the crematorium. *"And what was her favourite?"* I asked, out of curiosity. *"Keep the home fires burning"* was the innocent reply. *"Oh dear"*, I replied, in the most kindly tone I could manage, *"Don't you think the words would be a little misplaced given where we will be?"* *"Oh yes, I see what you mean"* said he rather abashed. After some discussion we decided on another favourite of hers, "We'll gather lilacs in the spring again."

I consider that a word about the office of churchwarden is in order. I have been fortunate in having reliable, committed wardens in every parish in which I have served. Some have been the more practical "hands on" type around the church, others the more capable of helping with general administrative work.

The Church needs talents of all kinds to be offered in the building up of his Kingdom. As parish priests we are "birds of passage". Churchwardens and their successors are permanently responsible for the "aviary" of God. In these days of long vacancies in parishes much of the keeping up of morale revolves around the ability of the wardens to rally the troops and prove their leadership of the congregations they represent. I am not sure whether, when it comes to considering both wardens "in tandem" as responsible leaders, that the Church of England has a more sensible arrangement for choosing churchwardens than the one that we adopt in Wales. In England both wardens are the nominations of the people at the Vestry Meeting. In Wales one warden is the appointment of the incumbent, the other elected by the people. The result of our system can be that the Vicar's Warden is considered to be on a somewhat higher plane than the People's Warden. Perhaps more importantly, the Vicar's Warden may feel a little inhibited that, as the chosen person of the Vicar, he or she has a moral duty to support what the incumbent says or does, when in fact he or she may think otherwise. With both wardens elected this dilemma would not arise. This comes down to the prevailing attitude towards clergy as a class of people. There still lurks in Wales, (and no doubt in England also) an over-reliance on the role of clergy and the tendency to put them on a pedestal where they do not wish to be, nor should be. With the recent movement towards lay leadership and lay ministry of all kinds that was unheard of 50 years ago, the age of the "cassock clingers" has hopefully had its day! Our Holy Eucharist service proclaims, *"We all share One Bread!"* That means that the Church, which is the Body of Christ, has no "pedestals" or "stools", only seats for the respective functions of priest and people to be occupied in God's service and to His glory.

As "would-be artist" I conclude these sweeping brush-strokes across my canvas by recommending three items of equipment which I have found indispensable on my pilgrimage through life. Indeed I hold them as desirable for all who wish to serve the Lord in the life of his Church. The first is ADAPTABILITY. This does not mean being all things to all people as though we are kites blown about wherever a gust of wind takes us, but sensitively drawing on God's wisdom to discern what each situation on its merit demands of us and praying his strength will help us meet the need of that situation. The Psalmist puts it well when he says, *"I will direct thee in the way wherein thou shalt go; I will counsel thee and guide thee with my eye."*

The second is PERSEVERANCE. This does not mean a dogged, hand to the grindstone gritting of the teeth as we grapple with all life's struggles and appear as though life itself is a burden too hard to bear, but a joyful determination to do what we know the Holy Spirit has called us to do and see it through to the end knowing that *"we run with perseverance the race that is set before us"* as the writer of Hebrews puts it. I have been involved in many circumstances that test my ability to persevere, even after retiring.

The third is OPTIMISM which I would prefer to describe as HOPEFULNESS. The reason why I hesitate to use the first word is that we associate an optimist with one who has his head in the clouds and is dismissive of the things happening all around him. Being hopeful however is having a solid basis for our trust in God's care to help us face the reality of the here and now. It is this hope that encourages the apostle to proclaim to his young partner in the Gospel, Timothy, *"We have a hope in the living God who is Saviour of all men."* It is the hope that inspires all Christians today to sing that hymn, *"All my hope in God is founded."*

And so my story comes to a close. My pilgrimage as the valley boy that went west continues now at its now gentler pace, even though it takes me hither and thither on Sundays. I regret that my pilgrimage as a parish priest has been so tiresomely linked to church buildings along the way, but without them, although life would be more comfortable, would it be tolerable or possible? I am so very grateful for the loving relationships that I have shared with two long-suffering and supportive partners in life, without whom I would surely have been a lesser human being. I am greatly uplifted in the knowledge that, in travelling west, I was not searching like the trail-blazers of the Wild West for good fortune to smile on him. Rather, I was grasping more firmly the prize that knows no price which is the privileged possession of all who follow Jesus Christ, wherever they may happen to be.

APPENDIX

I append the following hymns that I have put together over recent years as a pastime. They are hymns that have been composed to meet the need of a certain occasion, hence their titles. The tunes are only suggestions based on what I considered to be familiar to most congregations. If you decide to arrange for them to be sung in church the priest or minister must obtain copyright from me. You may wish just to use them as prayers. Either way, I wish you every blessing as you praise God with heart and voice.

HYMN FOR THE NEW MILLENNIUM   Tune   Fulda

1.　Lord of each age, we name you King;
　　God of all time and space to raise;
　　You whose rich blessings now we sing
　　Fill heart and voice with joy to praise.

2.　Lord of our lives whose pains you share,
　　We seek your aid in danger's hour,
　　Our greatest longings, wants and cares
　　We now entrust to your loving power.

3.　Lord of the world, we crave your reign
　　To come in justice, truth and peace;
　　May lands unite your love to claim,
　　From shameful greed then be released.

4.　Lord Christ, we celebrate today
　　The birth that faith and hope restores,
　　Come, let your Spirit's endless ray
　　Shine on our path for evermore.

CHRISTINGLE HYMN   Tune   Sing Hosanna

1.   The christingle begins with the orange
     Like the world that the Lord God made;
     For Creation is full of his glory,
     All around we see his love displayed.

CHORUS   Sing Christingle! Sing Christingle!
                Sing Christingle! It's the light of Christ!
                Sing Christingle! Sing Christingle!
                Sing Christingle, Light of Christ!!

2.   The sultanas and nuts serve a purpose
     They speak of goodness to us always;
     For the fruits of the earth in their season
     To our comfort, let us now give praise.

3.   The red band is a symbol of suffering
     Of a Saviour on Calvary's tree;
     But the wonderful news all can share in
     Is that there he died for you and me.

4.   But the candle is first and is foremost;
     Tis through this we see day through night;
     And the message it brings to Christ's followers
     Is that He is our true Hope and Light.

WEDDING HYMN   Tune   Plaisir D'Amour

1.   God's name is Love,
     And those he calls his own
     Are one in him till at length
     They surround his throne.

2.   In love we come
     Today to praise that name;
     In hearts aflame with his Spirit
     In love remain.

3.   God's love we share
     In lives joined into one;
     We show in faith his compassion
     Till life's day's done.

4.   God's name is Life,
     The life from sin set free
     May we who share life as one
     In that name agree.

5.   His name brings peace
     Midst life's distress and tears
     When pain, strife, clamour beset us
     Casts out each fear.

6.   God's name we claim
     In honour glorified;
     While we rest safe 'neath his arms
     Love is magnified.

HARVEST HYMN Tune Kocher 7,6,7,6

1.   Good Lord, who stirs the blackbird
   To sing at break of day;
   O stir us now to worship
   And bless us as we pray.

2.   Good Lord, who calls the flowers
   To bloom in bright array;
   Now call us so to travel
   With you on life's highway.

3.   Good Lord, who decks the hedgerows
   With summer cloak so green;
   Now clothe us in great measure
   With joy and peace serene.

4.   Good Lord, who paints each bright star
   To shine throughout their spheres;
   Inflame our hearts with courage
   And banish sin and fears.

5.   Good Lord, who rules the oceans
   Becalming storm-tossed wave;
   So grant us through life's tumults
   Your guiding hand to save.

6.   All thanks to you, the Giver
   Of rain and tiny seed;
   In lives to you we offer
   Each thought and word and deed.

CHRISTMAS CAROL Tune "Christmas Carol" H. Walford Davies

1. O come and see in stable bare
   The Son of God most high;
   A humble manger for a bed
   Whose home is in the sky;
   As cruel blows the wind without
   He sleeps secure within;
   Yet in our hearts we name him King
   Who life eternal brings.

2. What joy is ours, in ox's stall
   This helpless Child divine!
   The Maker of the stars and seas
   Come down to Palestine!
   No love that in a family
   Can with this love compare,
   That God was found in human form
   For us His life to share.

3. The Christmas bells send out their chime
   This great truth to proclaim,
   In stained glass window's shining hue
   The glory still remains.
   No carolling in candle glow, no holly on the tree
   Can stir us like the angels' song,
   "He comes to set us free."

EASTER HYMN   Tune   **Vulpius**

1.   Come, faithful souls, with one accord,
Bless and adore the risen Lord
For death laid low and life restored.
Hallelujah! Hallelujah! Hallelujah!

2.   Souls bound by Satan's mighty chain
Now are released to hope again;
Tomb flung away, in power he reigns,
Hallelujah! Hallelujah! Hallelujah!

3.   Praise him whose love can never die;
Victor is he in home on high,
Yet in our hearts in peace abides,
Hallelujah! Hallelujah! Hallelujah!

4.   Buried with him in death, we bring
Lives that are bound to Christ our King,
Anthems of joy for aye we sing,
Hallelujah! Hallelujah! Hallelujah!